Hydroponics

A Beginner's Guide to Learn the Principles of Hydroponics and Aquaponics for Higher Quality Gardening. Improve your Greenhouse Productivity and Grow Healthy Fruits and Vegetables

By

Thomas Watergreen

Table of contents

Introduction

Many persons have similar expectations of gardens owned by vegetarians. They expect to see a garden having rows and mounds with some dirt added (the traditional way), but this is not the modern way to do gardening anymore. As the world keeps evolving, everything changes along with it, including farming methods. Many people are moving past the old long traditional method of rows and mounds farming. They are now focused on a more ingenious way to do gardening for consumption. A lot of the fresh fruits and vegetables that we get in stores are now cultivated with the new way of farming called the Hydroponic method of farming. This hydroponic way of growing vegetables and fruits has proven to be very useful, especially during winter and in colder climates.

Hydroponics is one of the methods used to grow crops without using the soil. The plants are usually grown in rows and columns; however, it is just like traditional gardening, but this time in a much more dynamic form. This time, they have their roots fitted in water and not on dirt.

This idea came from an innovative search to get the difference between soil and dirt. The food for the plant does not come from dirt, against popular beliefs; it comes from mixture substances that are in the soil, such as compost, fertilizers, and broken down plants. The actual truth is that plants that are grown hydroponically would grow faster and much healthier than plants in the soil. This is because they don't have to fight any diseases that would have been in the soil. All food and water they need are given to them directly to their roots, and this is done continuously.

The art of growing plants in a hydroponic medium may be done on a large scale or not. And it is usually straightforward to do it than you might think.

There are some kits that you must have to have your hydroponic medium ready successfully. There are several do it yourself medium that you can efficiently operate for your use.

It is quite simple, and in different ways, it is way simpler than when you grow plants on the soil. There are lots of factors to look out for when you plant on the soil. The essentials to growing a healthy plant, you will understand that the three basic things they need are water, food, and air. As soon as you understand this fact, then you will be able to give them just the things that they need and removing all excesses that may affect their health.

The plants that are grown on hydroponics would thrive on just nutrient alone, and this can act as excellent support for the root and the plant system.

Advantages of the hydroponic methods of growing plants

With this method, you will be able to grow plants per square foot in the hydroponic garden; this is because the roots are usually given directly the nutrients that are needed to grow. Hence there is no form of competition for the space of roots or even the availability of nutrients. This will invariably lead to a high yield than planting with the soil.

The growth rate of the plant will increase; this is because they would be given the nutrients they need to grow in just the exact proportions. And this can boost the speed at which it utilizes the available nutrients.

The root of the plant will remain small, and this can give the plant more opportunity to spend much of its energy on the growth of its leaves and fruits, which are the needed part of the plant.

To get this best, you will have to follow these steps on a routine basis, and just by doing this, you will be able to see your plant thrive. And as soon as you get accustomed to the system, it then becomes as easy as a snap. You should also be aware that anything can be grown hydroponically. However, you should have at the back of your mind that some plants will do well than other plants in the hydroponic system. Tomatoes, peppers, lettuce, and spinach, and different flowers of all types can be grown in the system too.

How Does Hydroponics Work?

There are many ways in which plants are grown hydroponically; one method sets the plants erect in a plastic trough, and then the nutrients are placed into the solution in trickles through the root. This process is called the nutrient film technique; this nutrient is more like a conveyor belt because it continually goes past the root hence giving to them all the nutrients they need.

Also, you can grow the plant with a system to support the roots. This can be either Rockwool, vermiculite, or sand; these systems will usually act as a sterile option for soil. Often Aeroponics is explained like the roots are suspended inside the container that is filled with humid air. This way, the roots are growing in an abundant aerosol that is clouded with minerals. You can grow virtually any plant in the Water Culture, but then some plants will do better than some other plants; plants such as lettuce, herbs, and tomatoes would do well when planted in a hydroponic system.

Chapter 1: What Is Hydroponics?

1.1 What Is Hydroponic Gardening?

To all flower lovers who are planning to grow plants without soil, Hans von Berlepsch's appeal to "first of all study the theory" in full so as not to remain handicraftsmen for the whole life fully applies. This is true: everyone can purchase a special hydro pot, plant a beautiful plant in it, and take care of it following the instructions. However, in this case, there is no understanding of the relationships and hidden processes. To know the life processes of a plant well, this is clearly not enough, and it is such knowledge that is of the most significant value to us.

1.2 How Hydroponic Gardening Works - Growing Plants In and Without Soil

The primary factor - the soil - has been closely associated with agricultural production since time immemorial. In the broadest circles, it has been taken for granted even today that humus-containing natural soil, with its infinite variety of small and tiny organisms, is an essential condition for normal plant growth. We affirm that we can do fine without soil, and we will try to substantiate this statement.

For someone who has a plot of land for growing plants, the expression "soil ripeness" should be well known. With the nutrient-rich, ripe soil, the highest yields are obtained. Let us try to examine the ripe soil and the "normal" soil more closely in general to determine the conditions under which the plants develop most luxuriantly.

We consider the soil, that is, the upper loose populated by plants, a weathered layer of the globe, as a three-phase system, characterized by always present three phases: solid, liquid, and gaseous. Any soil can serve as a habitat and a source of nutrition for plants only in the case of a favorable combination of these three phases.

In ripe soil, the ratio of these quantities, i.e., solid, liquid, and gaseous phases, corresponds to a proportion of 50:25:25. Half of the soil volume thus consists of a porous space, which again is half-filled with soil solution and a half with soil air.

Solid soil constituents are predominantly solid inorganic materials. They are a product of weathering rocks with sizes from large fragments to the smallest particles. The organic part of the solid phase of the soil consists of the decomposition products of animals and plant organisms and the metabolic products of animals and microorganisms.

Natural soil is characterized by an endless variety of microorganisms that feed on the organic part of the soil. During this process, organic matter is wholly decomposed to form water and carbon dioxide, and the mineral food products of plants contained in the organic mass are converted into a form in which they can be absorbed by plants. Along the way, microorganisms, due to complex chemical and biological processes, contribute to the further weathering of inorganic particles, and new quantities of plant nutrients are released. Thus, we can state that the totality of organisms living in the soil fulfills a vital task in it - in combination with other factors (various weathering factors), continuously replenish the sources of nutrients in the soil.

During the so-called mineralization process just described plant nutrients such as nitric, phosphoric and sulfuric acids, etc., and are formed, which form salts with calcium, potassium, magnesium, etc.

The formation or release of vital trace elements (boron, copper, manganese, etc.) occurs in precisely the same way. All these chemical compounds essential for plant nutrition can be absorbed by them only with water, which serves as a means of dissolution and movement. Thus, soil moisture is a nutrient solution containing substances that are essential for plant nutrition. It must again be emphasized that the source of plant nutrition is only the soil solution with the nutrients it contains. On the contrary, organic compounds can be considered as sources of nutrients only after their complete microbiological decomposition. (Organic matter, of which the dry matter of plants is about 95%, it is formed by itself from water and carbon dioxide with the help of solar energy. They are never extracted from the soil in the finished form. The soil only supplies the missing 5% of mineral compounds).

It should not be forgotten that water is necessary not only as a solvent and a vehicle, it also serves as a nutrient in the construction of plants and, besides, performs other various psychophysiological tasks (for example, promotes the swelling of colloids, etc.) No plant is not able to grow without water, and in general, life without it is impossible. Lack of soil moisture can significantly reduce yield.

Now about the soil air. It should, apparently, play a rather large role, because we always strive to promote its aeration by cultivating the soil. This is understandable given that every living thing breathes, and therefore, requires oxygen. This, of course, applies not only to plant roots and storage organs (tubers, bulbs, etc.) but also to other organisms in the soil. If the surface of the soil coalesces so that regular air exchange is hampered, or if excess water in the soil displaces the soil air, then the underground parts of the plants suffer from a lack of oxygen. In this case, animal organisms inhabiting the soil can compete with cultivated plants to oxygen consumption. Therefore, we must always take care of it.

From the preceding, we can conclude about the conditions necessary for growing full-fledged plants also without soil.

First of all, each plant requires a habitat in which it can be fixed by roots. And here it does not matter at all whether the roots will be in the mass of rice husks, gravel, peat chips, or coal slag. The substrate performs only a physical role and has nothing to do with plant nutrition. For this, a so-called nutrient solution is used.

A nutrient solution, as a natural source of plant nutrition, should contain all the compounds that a plant needs for lush growth and fruiting in the right form, sufficient concentration, and in proper proportions. Countless experiments with nutrient solutions have made it possible to clarify the needs of well-known cultivated plants so well that we can now make recipes for nutrient solutions. Periodic resumption of the solution and its regular monitoring and replenishment of the loss of individual components allows us to provide adequate nutrition to our pets.

Microorganisms inhabiting natural soil are completely redundant when growing plants without soil due to the use of a ready-made nutrient solution. From it, plants receive all the food in an already digestible form, and there is no need for its processing. The nature of this or that artificial substrate does not need any influence from soil microorganisms. (In natural soil, we are very grateful to the organisms living in the soil for the formation of so-called soil aggregates.) Thus, we can choose materials that, after appropriate preliminary processing, will correspond in their structure to the structure of ripe soil (50% solid particles, 50% porous space). By this, we already provide a reasonably good supply of oxygen to the root growth zone, and thanks to the method of supplying the nutrient solution — and we will learn more about this below — we can achieve a really optimal supply of air.

Summarizing the above, we state that plants can be grown without any soil. You only need to be able to observe and simulate the processes occurring in the soil. If we can provide our pets with everything that is in fertile soil, then we will achieve the same goal - the lush growth of healthy plants.

1.3 Why Plant Growth May Stop

If this happens, then you should immediately remember the "law of the minimum." What is meant by this?

Let us allow ourselves a little digression and imagine the walk of a family with small and older children. The family moves quite slowly forward because the short legs of the children, perforce, determine the pace of movement. A little imagination, and we will be able to formulate a law: the speed of the family is limited by the feet of the youngest child - it is a limiting factor!

In the development of plants, similar circumstances play a role. A plant doesn't develop because of growth factors available in the optimal amount, but because those same factors are absent, therefore, are at a minimum. For this reason, even the best fertilizers and irrigation will not give anything if you try to grow some light-loving plant in the dark...

The fact that there is not enough growth factor that determines the boundaries of a plant's development even when there are optimal quantities of other factors is called the "Law of the Minimum."

One smart and humorous gardener taught his students to always remember the five letters if they want the plants to grow. He had in mind the capital letters of the names of factors that are crucial for plant growth: light, water, air, heat, and nutrition.

If a plant is provided with all these factors, it can fully manifest itself; that is, its growth will be most magnificent.

Using the method of growing plants without soil, we can directly affect the supply of plants with water, nutrition, and, with a known skill, bring it closer to optimal. However, we should never forget about other factors - light, warm air, and, as far as possible, we will take into account the unique needs of individual decorative and healthy plants. These factors should not be limiting. There is a lot of good literature available for a more detailed look at these issues.

1.4 The Basics of Hydroponics

What do your plants require?

Both plants need the right conditions to reach their full potential. Plants grown by systems of hydroponics are no exception to this fundamental rule. As their soil relatives, they require adequate light of the appropriate wavelengths, an adequate temperature, and adequate supply of water, enough oxygen, mineral nutrients, and structural support.

An adequate light of the right wavelengths is essential for the plant's survival at its growth stage. Plants use a lot of light every day, at least 8 to 12 hours, to generate carbon dioxide and water. The green color of plants, chlorophyll, absorbs the sunlight, and uses its energy to synthesize these carbs.

This process is called photosynthesis and is the basis for the survival of life in all plants. As animals and people eat plants, it can also be viewed as the source of our lives. Artificial lighting is generally a poor substitute for sunlight, as most indoor lights do not produce a mature crop in enough intensity.

High-intensity lamps such as high-pressure sodium lamps will supply over 1000 foot light candles. The hydroponic gardener can very effectively use these lamps in areas where sunlight is not adequate.

Nevertheless, the machinery and lamps are typically too costly for a small commercial company to operate. There must be ample spacing between plants, as this ensures that every plant gets enough light in the growing room.

For example, plants of tomatoes cut into one stalk must be planted to give 4 square feet per plant, while seedless cucumbers of 7 to 9 square feet and seeded cucumbers of approximately 8 square feet must be permitted in Europe.

The salad plants must be 7 to 9 centimeters apart in the row and 9 centimeters between rows. Most other vegetables and flowers should be planted at the same distance as for the traditional greenhouse.

For the plant to grow naturally, suitable temperature is needed. Too high or too low temperatures can cause uneven development and decreased performance. Summer and most flowers are best grown between 60 ° and 80 ° F, while winter vegetables such as spinach and lettuce tend to have temperatures between 50 ° and 70 ° F.

Appropriate water is usually not a concern in the use of a hydroponic system, since water-containing solution nutrients are the basis of hydroponics. However, some systems can cause insufficient watering, with the resulting adverse results for your plants.

Ebb and flow systems not tested on a reasonable basis can run short of nutrients, as can continuously flow systems in their storage tanks. Most, if not all, automated hydroponic systems can have catastrophes unless closely monitored.

Blocked or burst pipes or pump failure can lead to a lack of nutrient flow, resulting in dry roots and severe damages to or even deaths of your plants together with extreme lighting and the appropriate ambient temperature in the growing room.

Oxygen is a fundamental requirement for most living things. Plants require breathing oxygen to take water and nutrients. There usually is enough oxygen in soil environments, but plant roots in water use the supply of dissolved oxygen quickly.

This may harm or even destroy the plant without the provision of additional air. The bubbling air through the solution is a common way of ventilating the nutrient. Continuous flow and aeroponic systems typically do not require additional oxygen.

Many green plants require mineral nutrients. To order to survive, they must consume certain minerals from their roots. Minerals are provided by the soil and the application of fertilizers such as manure and compost in modern horticulture.

The large quantities of nitrogen, phosphorus, potassium, calcium, magnesium, and sulfur are required, and only tiny quantities of nitrates, iron, manganese, zinc, copper, molybdenum, and chlorine are needed.

The soil surrounding the growing plant normally provides support. Nevertheless, a plant grown with hydroponics must be artificially assisted. Typically this is achieved by string or stakes. You can buy cheap automatic string rollers to help your plants as they grow. This reduces the tedious task of continuing to adjust strings in rapidly growing plants.

Chapter 2: Pros and Cons

2.1 Pros and Cons - The Different Types of Hydroponic Systems

For everything to be calm at the home hydro farm, you need to know what advantages and disadvantages of different types of hydroponic systems have. The secret to the success of any undertaking is in choosing the right tools. It is unlikely that you can hammer a nail with the help of a banana. In progressive gardening, such a rule is present everywhere, including when choosing the type of hydroponic system. Each system has its pros and cons, which are worth paying attention to, so as not to fall into frustration.

2.2 Wick System

The wick is lowered into a nutrient solution, which rises up under the action of physical laws. The so-called passive system works wonders in the context of the relevance of the motto "cheap, but it works."

Pros:

- **Availability**. I took a container, poured a substrate - you can plant plants. Hydroponics for dummies;

- **Minimum cash costs for maintenance**. There is no technology - there are no problems with sensors, programs, and complex systems for providing plants with necessary substances. We need only the initiative of a cheerful water-carrier feedman;

- **Without a feed pump**. Since physics is the main driving force of the process, then additional assistance for the supply of nutrients to the roots of plants is not necessary.

Disadvantages:

- **Limited access to oxygen to water or solution**. It can cause a whole bunch of problems - stale water, problems with the root system, and so on.

- **Slow growth**. An independent plant cannot fully grow in breadth and height as a beginner would like if he had seen enough of the giant strawberry bushes on other hydroponic farms;

- **No nutrient recycling**. And why? That's right; because there is no pump. There is nothing to add.

2.3 Deepwater Crop System (DWC)

Higher than passive systems, but not having all the charms of hi-tech and engineering peaks, choice. A simple device, but with a "whistle" - a compressor that delivers oxygen to the nutrient solution, nourishing the root system. Which, in turn, is located in a mesh pot and installed in the lid of the tank with a nutrient solution.

Pros:

- The cheapest option from active systems. Savings - a necessity in a precarious American economy;

- Ease of setup and reliability. Based on the preceding, an undeniable plus for advanced beginners;

- Without a feed pump. The same plus as in the wick system;

- Reliable, due to the small number of brittle elements;

- A decent supply of solution guarantees the safety of your plants;

- Everything is growing and fast.

Disadvantages:

- Risk of root rot with insufficiently regular cleaning.

- With a high level of solution and excessive over moistening, the likelihood of decay of the root neck is high;

- The need to continually replenish the tank. A regular run for water and nutritious mixtures is a good help for losing weight, but not for progressive crop production.

2.4 Periodic Flooding System

A method that is also striking in its simplicity. Plants can be placed on top of each other, and the liquid flowing from one pot gets into another. Simple and tasteful. Of course, you can make an advanced option, with valves and sensors, which will allow you to control the liquid level in the substrate, which is suitable for the hydroponics and his wards.

Pros:

- Availability. To make an average hydroponic installation, you do not need to order tons of equipment and spend a lot of time choosing a manufacturer and understand a billion nuances;

- Low costs. The simplicity of the technology entails a small amount of money for maintenance;

- Good saturation with a nutrient solution. Nutrients pass through the entire substrate. Vigorous growth and high productivity available.

Disadvantages:

- Like any reversible system, there is a risk of contamination of the solution with pathogens'

- The risk of mold and other "water" weeds. If there is a lot of water, then parasites will undoubtedly appear, which will live there freely;

- Technical malfunctions can lead to a decrease in yield. If any valves get stuck, or the water separation system itself is de-energized, then goodbye to regular watering, and as a result, caput to the mountains of vegetables.

2.5 Drip Irrigation System

This is hydroponics, "as it is." A description is not required. However, this system has its advantages and disadvantages. First of all, it is worth noting that drip irrigation does not require particular intervention in the process by humans. But it is worth decently investing in so that everything works like a clock.

Pros:

- The nutrient solution goes to "5+ stars". The system is so good that it is used by most hydroponic firms in the West;

- A sufficient supply of oxygen to the root system. This means that there should not be any problems with the circulation of nutrients. Consequently, the seedlings will grow and turn into the pride of a gardener, just as per the instructions.

Disadvantages:

- The biggest minus is the need for regular cleaning to eliminate blockages in the irrigation system. And a similar method is fraught with the development of mold on the roots and containers.

2.6 Aeroponics

"Ferrari" hydroponics. The most effective method for growing vegetables, fruits, and other flora on an industrial scale. But for a home farm, it suits well enough, although you have to sweat to understand all the intricacies of technology. Although the profit from this is rather significant.

Pros:

- Maximum absorption of nutrients. Due to aeroponic technology, as many substances as the plant needs come to the roots;

- Efficient use of space. You can arrange the trays at least in three layers. There will be no empty space for sure. So, the harvest will be such that before spring is enough.

Disadvantages:

- Blockages, blockages, and again blockages. Nowhere to go from them. Therefore, you need to regularly check all nodes, contacts, and sensors. You can say goodbye to personal life and cheating;

- Aeroponics is poorly suited for thick nutrient mixtures. This cannot be called a drawback, but for the ignorant, it can serve as a motivation to throw crop production into the far corner along with cross-stitch and modeling.

Choosing the Right Hydroponic System

Be that as it may, hydroponics requires a thorough study of the theoretical part. Well, the choice of a hydroponic system depends entirely on personal preferences, your scale of operation, and the cost you are willing to spare in your hydroponic operation.

Chapter 3: Different Types of Hydroponic Garden

After we have received the necessary basic knowledge, we can proceed to the construction of structures. However, before that, we will get acquainted with the meaning of some terms to understand clearly all the literature related to this issue.

3.1 Clarification of Understandings

Hydroponics is a collective concept for all growing methods in which a plant is rooted in a relatively thin layer by a large part of the organic substrate. The substrate itself is laid on a perforated base, which, in turn, is lowered into a trough (or tray) filled with a nutrient solution. Plant roots penetrate through the substrate layer and the openings of the base into the solution and thus satisfy the plant's need for food and water.

We will see that using this principle, it is possible to build both very small and gigantic installations. Often they are called aquatic cultures in tanks, vessels, racks, etc.

The term hydroculture we can, if not literally, then in meaning, translate as a gravel culture. This method is distinguished primarily by the fact that with it, plants take root in solid layers of gravel (up to 40 cm thick). The provision of a nutrient solution, in this case, can occur following two primary principles.

3.2 Backwater Enriched Hydroponic Gardens

In a backwater method, the bottom of the gravel is continuously in a nutrient solution that can rise through the capillaries. Plant roots, of course, can grow unhindered down to the level of a nutrient solution, and they very actively use this opportunity.

With the method of periodic flooding (or humidification), the nutrient solution is supplied to the tank or trough at regular intervals.

Moreover, most of the gravel layer is literally flooded and can be completely saturated with the solution (due to the porosity of the substrate).

If then the solution is again removed (drained or sucked) and completely fresh air enters the porous space of the substrate layer, then the supply of oxygen to the plant roots becomes really optimal.

Now, let's get to work. First, we will get acquainted with several types of backwater-style hydroponic gardens that have already gained great popularity.

3.3 Automatic Watering Flower Box Batteries

This installation works on the principle of a constant backwater. Let's start right from the point: would it not be wrong to get rid of the need to water the flowers daily to eliminate the overflow of pots and crates that constantly occur during watering, in which walls, window sills, and cornices get dirty and willy-nilly arises. So, every active amateur can do this at home. What will be described below does not go on sale, and you need to do everything by yourself.

To build a battery of flower boxes with automatic watering, waterproof boxes or boxes are required. It is best if it is asbestos-cement or metal boxes, but both are not so easy to get it, and their cost is relatively high. You can also use wooden drawers, which can be turned into waterproof with phenol-free plastic films.

First, take asbestos cement boxes, which can be purchased everywhere, and cover them with a layer of bitumen paint to eliminate the possibility of exchange reactions with a nutrient solution in the future.

Then in the boxes on both sides, you need to make holes whose diameter corresponds to the diameter of the rubber plugs we prepared in advance.

These plugs must be drilled so that glass tubes with a clearance of 12 mm can be inserted into them. After the tube plugs are carefully fitted to the openings in the drawers, we connect the tubes of adjacent drawers with short pieces of rubber hose. A piece of a glass tube bent at right angles is inserted into the last stopper, which serves as a control indicating the height of the solution level, and if it is turned 180 ° down, then also to drain the solution. This ends the device system's centralized supply of boxes with nutrient solution.

Next, we need a suitable feed tank for a solution with a hermetically sealed neck. A clean canister or can with a screw cap and a sealing ring is quite suitable for this. They are isolated with ordinary bituminous paint, pouring it in and turning the vessel so that the paint covers all the walls. A natural job, which may require outside assistance, is steaming at the base of the canister or can of mortar tube (inner diameter of the tube is 12 mm). After that, you can begin the installation of the entire installation.

To get started, stock up on a rubber hose long enough to attach the feed tank to the first drawer. Then, at a distance of 10-15 cm from the solution tank, we cut the hose and insert a T-shaped glass tube (12 mm in diameter) into the cut ends so that its long endpoints up and slightly to the side. Why this is done will be clear from a further discussion of the processes that occur after filling the tank and supplying the solution.

Using the clamp, we block the hose between the tank and the T-pipe and fill the tank with a nutrient solution. After the tank plug is screwed, you can remove the clip. What will happen?

The solution will begin to flow into all the boxes because the replacement air may enter the reservoir through the open end of the T-tube.

The solution level in all the boxes will rise slowly and evenly until it reaches the open end of the T-pipe, as is the case with any communicating vessels. After that, the flow of solution into the boxes instantly stops. This phenomenon is not difficult to explain: after the air from the outside ceases to enter the reservoir through the open end of the T-shaped tube, the solution cannot flow out. Otherwise, an airless space would be created in the tank.

Next, we should take care of such an arrangement of empty boxes so that the solution level in them is at the same height. It is also necessary to adjust the position of the T-shaped tube (its open upper end) so that the flow of the solution ceases when the solution in all the boxes is at the height of 2.5-3.0 cm. After that, the boxes can be filled with a substrate.

Larger gravel is laid at the very bottom with a 2 cm thick layer to ensure the free movement of water even in a wholly filled box. A thin layer of fibrous peat is placed on top of this gravel to prevent the filtration of small particles of the substrate to the bottom of the box. The rest of the space is filled with prepared gravel or clean peat chips. If plants are planned to be grown on gravel, then they must be supplied with a nutrient solution from the very beginning. If peat is chosen as the substrate, then when filling the boxes for every 10 liters of peat, you need to mix 30 g of standard full fertilizer. This basic fertilizer will be enough for the first 3-4 weeks, and during this period, only water is supplied from the tank to the boxes. Still, later they switch to the supply of a nutrient solution of normal concentration.

Anyone who strictly follows all these requirements will receive great satisfaction by observing the development of plants in their crates.

Flowers grow in them exceptionally well because they receive water and food in the required amount. Indeed, as soon as the level of the solution in the boxes, as a result of evaporation and use by plants, decreases so much that the open end of the T-shaped tube is entirely free, air will penetrate into the tank, and the liquid flowing out of it will again raise the level of the solution in all boxes, and this will be repeated until the solution remains in the tank.

Practice shows that, depending on the time of year, exposure, and type of plants, the flow rate of the solution is 0.5-2.0 liters per day per 1 meter of the length of the balcony boxes. Based on this value, we can easily calculate how often (depending on the capacity of the tank) you need to replace the solution. One tank can supply a solution of 5-6 flower boxes of normal size without difficulty.

Separate flower boxes, display cases, and terrariums

Flower showcases on hydroculture are not only a detail of the environment that provides a suitable habitat for plants, but they can also serve as a bookcase or a wine cellar, while terrariums on hydroculture provide an opportunity for lovers of these devices to decorate them with lushly growing ornamental plants

Such devices primarily require a waterproof, insulated bathtub whose length and width fully comply with our requirements. It should be such a depth that the substrate layer after filling was at least 25 cm thick. A perforated (also coated with insulating paint) pipe is laid along the entire length of the bathtub, designed to drain and accelerate the movement of the liquid when the solution is supplied and drained. In the place where the pipe rests on the edge of the bath, a drain tap is attached.

A showcase with a hydroculture is supplied in one of the corners with a vertical pipe segment serving as a control tube and a pipe for supplying a nutrient solution. The height of the solution level in the substrate is easily determined using a rod lowered into the control tube.

In a terrarium with a hydroculture, unlike a flower showcase, there is no tube for supplying the solution. Still, at the end of the drainage pipe, opposite the drain tap, a control tube bent at right angles with a diameter of 3 cm is mounted, which is also suitable for supplying the solution. Using this device located outside the bath, we can replace the nutrient solution without opening the terrarium for this.

At the bottom of the bathtub of a showcase or terrarium, a layer of rather large gravel is first poured, and the rest of the space is filled with an ordinary substrate (with a particle diameter of 2-10 mm). A 1/3 bath should always be filled with nutrient solution. The entire solution is changed every 2-3 weeks to have confidence in the constant availability of food for plants.

Such boxes can, of course, be used without automatic power. It is only necessary to provide an opening in the wall at the bottom in which a glass tube bent at right angles is fixed as control or drain. When this control tube shows that the solution level in the box has dropped significantly, the right amount is poured directly into the box. According to the same principle, very common flower showcases and terrariums on hydroculture are arranged.

3.4 Hydro Pots for Ornamental Plants

Such pots are used to grow potted plants without soil in an apartment or office. In the trading network, there are already quite numerous models of pots.

Hydroponic pots are those in which the root system of plants is immersed in a nutrient solution. In these pots for hydroculture, the habitat of plants is a flower pot filled with gravel. This pot is partially immersed in a nutrient solution so that porous gravel can provide the capillary uplift of the liquid.

An attentive reader will undoubtedly be able to quickly assemble water pots using simple means. To do this, you need the most capacious pot-bellied vase (of course, previously covered with an insulating layer, if necessary), into which a flower pot suitable in diameter, height, and shape are inserted. However, it can be made even simpler. For the first experiments, even such auxiliary materials as wide-necked glass jars, tin cans, and ordinary flower pots are sufficient. The essence of the matter is that the plants have the possibility of rooting and a sufficient supply of nutrient solution. You just need to always keep in mind the following:

- The outer pot, or vase, that is, the vessel for the nutrient solution, should be as spherical as possible so that the solution lasts for a longer period. In a pot of good capacity, the solution is replaced no more than two weeks later, and in the intervals, with strong evaporation, one or a maximum of two times the addition of ordinary water may be required. This is the work of care - a huge advantage of indoor floriculture without soil!

- In the nutrient solution, when given access to sunlight, algae settle very soon. Therefore, industrial-made hydro pots always have a special color that prevents the formation of algae. The development of algae is completely undesirable: they not only spoil the whole species but also compete with cultivated plants with regard to mineral salts and carbon dioxide. Therefore, using glass containers for your experiments, you need to wrap it with opaque paper or cover it with a layer of opaque paint from the outside.

3.5 The Periodic Flooding-Style Hydroponic Garden

So far, we have dealt with a technique in which the so-called backwater or recharge method is used. We also mentioned hydroponic pots. Let us turn now to the method of periodic "flooding."

Flooding can also be carried out on small installations with hydroculture. What is its essence? We repeat that with this method, the nutrient solution does not remain in the vessels for a long time, but is fed into them periodically. Due to this, good aeration of the root growth zone is achieved and, at the same time, plant nutrition is provided, since a porous substrate with good water-holding ability - gravel or peat - can be stored in abundance when the solution is poured. How to rationally use these advantages?

We will need two vessels, one of which will serve to grow plants, and the other - a reservoir for the nutrient solution.

The first experience will require only minor expenses. Two wide cylindrical buckets, which can be purchased everywhere, will serve as equipment for it. Each bucket is equipped with a drain pipe at the bottom, which is easy to make, securing it with a lock nut and equipping it with two rubber seals. After this, the buckets are connected with a rubber hose, and one of them is filled with a substrate, and the other with a nutrient solution, which must be completely replaced approximately every two weeks. The waste solution, still containing some nutrients, can be successfully used to feed other plants in the garden.

The next working step is to plant a young solution in a bucket with a substrate. In this case, you need to ensure that the bucket with the plant is always above the bucket with the solution. When we raise a bucket with a solution above a bucket with a plant, the solution enters the gravel through a hose, to which, in this case, when filling is added no more than 1/3 of peat, not to impede the movement of the solution. We repeat this operation, depending on the time of year, 2-3 times a day. Large plants in the warmest season require, of course, more food than small plants under a cloudy sky. When determining daily portions of the solution, this must be taken into account.

The flow of the solution can be further simplified by using a clamp or an overhead tap on the hose. Then you can leave the solution in the bucket with the plant for some time even after lowering the bucket with the solution. After about 20 minutes, when the porous gravel is completely saturated with the solution, the tap or clamp is loosened, and the solution again drains into an empty bucket. This simple and cheap device deserves attention because many lovers grow magnificent tomato plants in this way. They are most often abundantly covered with high-quality fruits.

It is hardly worth saying that, by the same principle, many similar installations can be built, for which each has enough of his own imagination. Let's move on to a more advanced amateur setup.

Chapter 4: Different Types of Hydroponics Gardens and How to Choose the EST for Us

There are hundreds of methods of hydroponic gardening. However, all these are combinations or variations of six basic types:

1. Water Culture

2. Wicks

3. Nutrient Film Techniques

4. Flood and Drains

5. Drips

6. Aeroponics

The following paragraphs give descriptions of the basic hydroponic systems and details of how each of them works.

4.1 The Water Culture

The Water Culture System is the simplest form of active hydroponics. The plants are commonly grown on a medium made of Styrofoam, and they grow directly from the nutrient solution. This system uses an air pump to supply oxygen to the plants' roots.

The Water Culture System is the best choice for growing water-loving plants such as lettuce. However, this system is not suitable for many long term or large plants, and these will not thrive using this system.

It is not expensive to make this type of hydroponic system. You can use an old aquarium or water container. It is the ideal set-up for a classroom. This makes it a popular choice for teachers and students.

4.2 The Wick System

Wicking is the simplest form of passive hydroponics. Passive means there are no moving parts in the system. The nutrient solution comes up through the wick from the reservoir and feeds the growing medium through this wick.

The growing mediums used for this system are coconut fiber, pro-mix, vermiculite, and perlite. It is an effective system for small plants because large plants tend to draw up the nutrient solution faster than the wicks can supply them.

4.3 Nutrient Film Technique

The Nutrient Film Technique or NFT is the most prevalent type of hydroponics. It is probably the cheapest and easiest to create. The benefit of this system is that no soil is used. The roots of the plants are suspended directly in water, and the nutrient solution is pumped into the water that covers the roots and drained back into a reservoir.

There is no need for a timer, and you do not have to replace the growing medium after every change of crop. The NFT usually makes use of a small plastic basket that has been designed to let the roots dangle into the nutrient solution. The only drawback is that when power outages and pump failures occur, the flow of solution is interrupted, and the roots tend to dry out easily.

4.4 The Flood and Drain System

This is known as "Ebb and Flow." It works by flooding the growing medium or tray with the nutrient solution and draining it back to the reservoir. This action is achieved by a submersible pump, which is connected to a pre-set timer.

The timer will trigger the pump to siphon the nutrient solution onto the tray. After this action, the timer will also shut the pump off so that the solution will ebb back. The gardener will set the timer to turn on several times during the day – the frequency will be dependent on several factors:

- Type of plant

- Size of plant

- Temperature

- Humidity

- Growing medium

The grow tray can be filled with different growing mediums. The most popular choices are rockwool, perlite, gravel, coconut fiber, and grow rocks. Most people use individual pots as trays.

The main challenge with the "Ebb and Flow" system is the susceptibility to power outages, pump failures, and timer failures. Some mediums like gravel and grow rocks will not hold the nutrient solution well enough, so the roots will dry out quickly when the cycle is interrupted. It is better to use

rockwool, coconut fiber, and pro-mix as they retain more water.

4.5 Drip System

The Drip System is the most widely used hydroponic system. It is set-up with a timer, a submerged pump, and a grow tray. The timer is set to turn the pump on to allow the nutrient solution to drip off directly onto the plants through a tiny drip line.

There are two kinds of Drip Systems: Recovery and Non-Recovery. In a Recovery Drip, the surplus nutrient solution that flows down is collected in a reservoir and re-used.

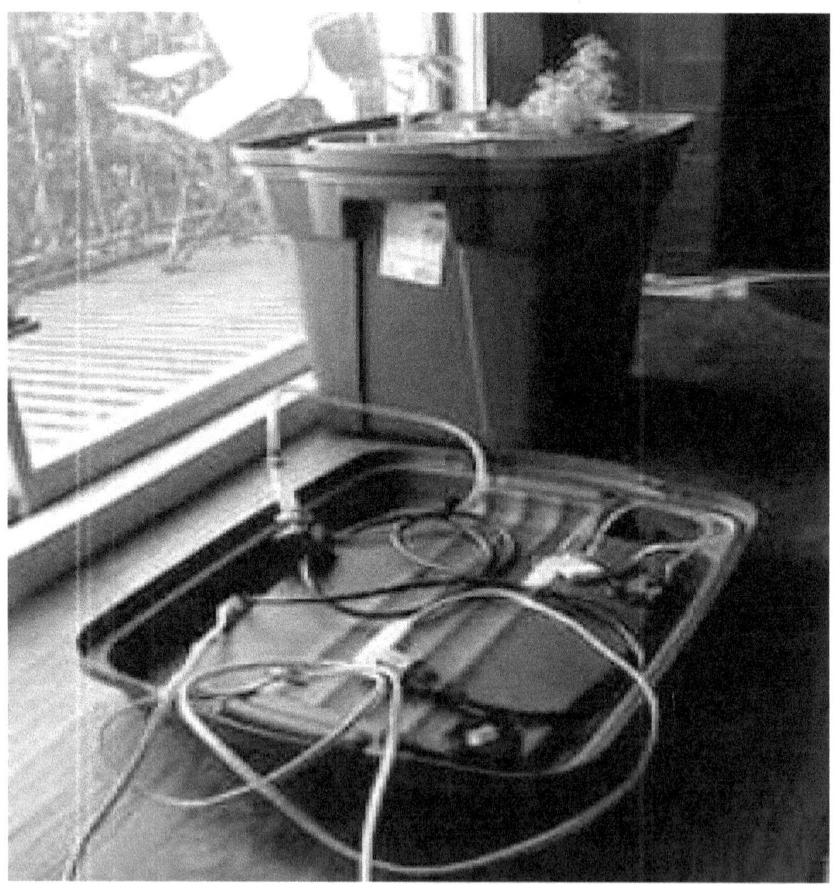

The Recovery Drip System is more efficient and less expensive. Apart from being able to re-use the excess nutrient solution, the system does not need precise control for the watering cycles. The timer needs to be more precise in a Non-Recovery Drip System, so the plants get enough of the nutrient solution, and there is minimal runoff.

The Recovery System requires more maintenance in recycling the solution back to the reservoir, and the pH and strength of the nutrient solution need to be preserved. This requires periodic testing and adjusting so that pH and strength levels do not shift. On the other hand, the Non-Recovery System needs less maintenance, as the solution is not re-used.

4.6 Aeroponics

A timer triggers the misting pump, similar to on the other hydroponic systems. The only difference is that there is a shorter cycle for the pump.

It is a quite delicate and complicated system. There should be no interruption to misting cycles. Otherwise, the roots will dry out quickly.

Chapter 5: Choosing the Best Lighting Medium for Your Hydroponic Plants

To upgrade the development of your plants, you have to have the privilege to develop lights. It is critical to make reference to now that despite the fact that glaring lights can be utilized to enhance characteristic light, they can't, all alone, give the range of light required by plants.

Metal Halide and High-Pressure Sodium Lights were created to discharge a range of light that impersonates the nature of light radiating from the sun. Metal Halide lights are the nearest you can get to daylight. They produce progressively a greater extent of blue light that is incredible for supporting vegetative development.

High weight sodium lights then again produce light that spreads a greater amount of the red-orange range. They last more, consume more splendid, and expend a lower measure of vitality than their metal halide partners, despite the fact that they produce a smaller range of light.

For the best outcomes, it is suggested that you join the utilization of the two kinds of lights to give light that is as close as conceivable to the full range of daylight. Moreover, you can utilize light reflectors and movers to cover a more extensive space with fewer lights.

5.1 Best Lighting Medium for Your Hydroponic Plants

To upgrade the development of your plants, you have to have the privilege to develop lights. It is critical to make reference to now that despite the fact that glaring lights can be utilized to enhance characteristic light, they can't, all alone, give the range of light required by plants.

Metal Halide and High-Pressure Sodium Lights were created to discharge a range of light that impersonates the nature of light radiating from the sun. Metal Halide lights are the nearest you can get to daylight. They produce progressively a greater extent of blue light that is incredible for supporting vegetative development.

High weight sodium lights then again produce light that spreads a greater amount of the red-orange range. They last more, consume more splendid, and expend a lower measure of vitality than their metal halide partners, despite the fact that they produce a smaller range of light.

For the best outcomes, it is suggested that you join the utilization of the two kinds of lights to give light that is as close as conceivable to the full range of daylight. Moreover, you can utilize light reflectors and movers to cover a more extensive space with fewer lights.

5.2 Fake Lighting Techniques

- **What Are Grow Lights?**

Lights are regularly utilized in applications where there is an absence of characteristic light, or extra light is required.

State, for instance, throughout the winter months, develop lights that can be utilized to supply extra-long stretches of light for plant development. It develops vegetables, and natural products develop inside too.

On a bigger scale, indoor cultivating tasks, develop lights can totally supplant direct daylight. Notwithstanding, develop lights don't generally need to imitate daylight precisely. In numerous applications, they can outflank daylight.

5.3 Sorts of Grow Lights

There are three essential sorts of develop lights accessible for indoor urban cultivating: Fluorescent develop lights, HPS or HID develop lights, and LED develop lights.

1. Fluorescent Grow Lights. Fluorescent develop lights are utilized for developing herbs and vegetables inside. They are two sorts, including fluorescent cylinders and Compact Fluorescent Lights (CFLs). Fluorescent cylinders come in a wide range of forces. They last more and are more vitality productive than glowing bulbs- - the normal bulbs that have been lighting homes for quite a long time. Bright light bulbs are flimsy and can, without much of a stretch, fit into little spaces. With respect to drawbacks, they require a weight to direct present, and the cylinders require a stand, instead of a traditional attachment.

Such necessities can add to the expense of the establishment.

Then again, CFLs have turned out to be progressively basic in family use and not simply in indoor urban cultivating. CFLs utilize just 20 to 30% of the vitality devoured by customary brilliant bulbs, and their life expectancy is six to multiple times longer.

They are by a long shot the least expensive among every one of the three significant sorts of develop lights. One outstanding favorable position with CFL bulbs is they don't emanate abundant heat, enabling ranchers to keep the lights nearer to the plants. This low warmth highlight makes it very vitality effective too.

2. HPS Grow Lights: High-Pressure Sodium (HPS) lights have developed in prominence and are surpassing fluorescent cylinders and bulbs. These lights are progressively normal among business and experienced indoor cultivators, and the innovation behind them is settled, effectively more than 75 years of age.

The issue with HPS is that it delivers a lot of warmth. All things considered, you should keep the lights a decent good ways from the plants. They require a lot of ventures to set up and keep up. Subsequently, HPS isn't suggested for little producers.

3. Driven Grow Lights: While the beginnings of LED innovation initially rose in the mid-1900s, the red and blue LEDs ideal for indoor cultivating started being utilized only preceding the 2000s.

Driven develop lights are the most vitality proficient among each of the three essential kinds of develop lights. These sources can be put more distant from plants while as yet delivering enough light without expending a lot of vitality. CFLs are practically half less proficient than LED develop lights. The warmth generation by LED develop lights is almost zero. Above all, LED performs best to make an ideal indoor condition to make practically any sort of nourishment.

The expense of LED lights is higher than the other two sorts, be that as it may. Also, laborers working in indoor ranches need to utilize eye insurance as LEDs can be unsafe to human eyes.

5.4 Characteristics of Lighting Techniques

The most straightforward approach to arrangement fake lighting for an indoor nursery is to recollect these dependable guidelines. 40 watts for each square foot for high light plants like tomatoes and peppers and 25 watts for every square foot for low light plants like lettuce and verdant plants.

This implies for an average 4' x 4' space, you would require 400 watts of lighting to develop low light adoring plants, and 600 watts of lighting to develop high return plants like huge tomato and pepper plants.

5.5 Joining Natural and Artificial Lighting Techniques

When thought about two unmistakable ways of thinking in agriculture, the line among indoor and open-air development is being obscured. Profoundly complex, all year nurseries are at the front line of this combination development as they use the accepted procedures of the two strategies in an innovative give and take. These tasks use the sun's vitality to control basic plant capacities while actualizing indoor developing advancements like light sensors, power outage covering frameworks, dehumidifiers, and mechanical radiators to mirror indoor ecological controls in open air settings.

5.6 Supplemental Lighting

Maybe the most essential innovative application in these current nurseries is that of supplemental lighting. In indoor planting, lighting is one of the most significant elements directing the result of a gathering.

Be that as it may, it is additionally perhaps the costliest component of activity, with an overhead of in any event $400 per unit for 1,000W twofold finished high weight sodium (HPS) lights and $800 per unit for similar light emanating diodes (LEDs). Taken to a business scale, this overhead can demonstrate very scary as it is exclusively dependent upon these counterfeit light sources to nourish each square inch of a gigantic nursery overhang. At that point, there is the galactic expense of running the lights in these huge scale set-ups. Some 10,000-square-foot distribution center developments have detailed power bills as much as $12,000 month to month.

Nonetheless, current nurseries utilize best practices from both indoor and outside development. With regards to lighting, this implies utilizing a cautious parity of daylight and supplemental light. It's changing the manner by which individuals develop crops outside.

5.7 High-Intensity Discharge (H.I.D.) Grow Lights

Metal halide lights were made to give a range as close as conceivable to that of the regular sunlight. This, combined with their force and energy productivity, makes them perfect for indoor gardening. The bulbs extend in size from 100-watt to 1000 watt with 400-watt and 1000-watt generally well known.

A wealth of blue light produced by metal halide makes them the most favorable light for propagation and vegetative growth, advancing short internodal length High-Pressure. Sodium lights don't emanate as wide a range as Metal Halides lights; however, they have numerous preferences, particularly when used related to halide.

Sodium lasts more and consumes more brilliant; however, they are still more energy productive. Progressively yellow/red shading in the range and less blue advances a higher blossom to-leaf proportion in blooming plants. H.P.S. lights are broadly used in business nurseries, where regular sunlight gives adequate blue. A mix of the two lights gives the best adjusted to the indoor grow room, mainly when used with a light mover. 430-watt Son-t Agro H.P.S. bulbs, which supply 30 additional watts than ordinary ones, are presently accessible. This additional light in the blue finish of the range is excellent news for indoor growers. If you are planning a "solitary light" grow room, you can, in any case, get the advantages of both halide and sodium light. High weight sodium "change bulbs," uniquely made to work with M.H. weights, are accessible in 400-watt and 1000-watt models. The bulbs can undoubtedly be exchanged varying, utilizing a similar balance and apparatus. The size of light required will rely upon the size of the growing region and the sort of plants you wish to develop.

High-light plants, for example, herbs and vegetables, will require somewhere in the range of 20 and 60-watt of light for each square foot of growing area. A 400-watt element halide in a three-foot by three-foot region will give 45-watt for each square foot, contrasted with 25-watt for every square foot in five foot by five foot grow room. A 1000-watt element halide in a five-foot by five-foot region will give 40-watt per sq. ft., contrasted with 20-watt for each square foot in a seven by seven-foot grow room.

Appropriate reflectors, light movers, and intelligent material on dividers significantly expand the force and effectiveness of these lights.

Most high-power lights can be run with either 120 volts (standard house current) or 240 volts (for example, used for electric dryer).

Electricity cost would be the equivalent, yet the last would draw a large portion of the amps enabling the producer to run twice the same number of lights on the equivalent electrical circuit.

Light timers are accessible for either voltage yet consistently verify that the amperage rating on the timer surpasses that of the light or lights.

Care ought to consistently be taken when introducing and utilizing H.I.D. lights.

Remote balances ought to be put securely off the beaten path where they can't be thumped over or sprinkled with water. Never keep your counterbalance on the floor if it gets wet. Introducing the installation and reflector is basic.

Find a stud in the roof close to the focal point of the developing zone. Screw a metal snare fit for holding 40 to 50 pounds into the stud and test its quality. Connect a 4' to 6' length of lightweight connection chain to the snare or snares over the installation and balance the apparatus from the roof snare at the ideal tallness. The connection bind enables you to raise and lower the effortlessly light when important. Hold the light close to the base and solidly, however tenderly, screw the bulb into the attachment. Interface the timer to the force source, plug the force string from the balance into the timer, which ought to be set in the "on" position. It might take as long as 30 seconds for the bulb to touch off and as long as five minutes to arrive at full brilliance. As the light touch off, they tend to gleam and change shading for a few minutes. This is very typical, particularly with halide bulbs, which may seem to change shading marginally during typical use. If the light doesn't touch off following 30 or 40 seconds, unplug it. After the force has been detached, check that the bulb is fastened the whole distance, and the timer is determined to the "on" position; all fittings or electrical associations are perfect.

NOTE: Never Open the Ballast Enclosure to check the electrical Wiring Yourself! H.I.D. capacitors can grip a charge significantly after the counterweight is unplugged.

When these focuses have been checked, attempt the light once more.

When a metal halide light is killed, it requires a 15 to 20 moment "cool down" period before it very well may be re-begun. If adequate cooling time isn't permitted, a "hot beginning" happens, and too much "hot beginnings" can genuinely influence the force and life span of the bulb. For best outcomes, supplant halide bulbs following one year of consistent use. High weight sodium lights require just 2 to 3 moment "chill off" period and need just be supplanted each a few years.

5.8 Light Movers

The most effective approach to utilize high power lights is to make them move inside the grow room. There are numerous favorable circumstances to this, and various ways it very well may be done. Moving the lights will dispense with plants' inclination to develop toward the light source and give light to zones that generally might be concealed.

Since the light can travel, it can pass very near the plants without consuming the leaves. Moving lights spread more zone than stationary ones, diminishing electricity costs and guaranteeing all the more even growth.

Greater power likewise enables plants to be set a lot of nearer together, extraordinarily expanding yield and quality. The size and state of your room will decide the kind of light mover that will be the best suite for your needs.

Lineal movers convey the light installation gradually along a track and back again during the light cycle. Most are six feet long, support a solitary light, and are prescribed when the growing zone is long and restricted.

Roundabout movers are best when the length and width of the room are comparable. They are intended to convey each one, two, or three lights, in a 360-point circle, naturally lighting a ten by ten-foot region. This width can be decreased, however, once in a while expanded.

Two arm and three-arm movers are generally known, with the last providing significantly more light per square foot. More power implies plants can be set a lot nearer together, greatly expanding yields.

Focal points of utilizing light movers:

1 - All the more even growth over a more significant territory

2 - Lights might be set nearer to crop

3 - Increment growth by 40%

4 - More grounded plant stems

5 - Check leaf concealing

6 - Round movers can climb to 3

7 - Amps

8 - 1 o 2 meter straight track support

9 - Single lights, augmentation packs are used for extra lights

Chapter 6: Pest Control

6.1 Pest Prevention and Control

You come to know about the various problems related to Hydroponics and how you can overcome them by applying varied techniques that can save the plants. You will read about how to prevent pests in your Hydroponics system and various control measures so that your garden will look attractive and impressive throughout the year.

In every greenhouse Hydroponic system, dozens of insect pests or you can say crop diseases affect it. No garden lover enjoys using agrichemical, but it becomes necessary to control that pest; otherwise, there is a risk of losing a crop.

In reality, the main reason why Hydroponic garden has access to a large number of insects or pests is an isolated area by which various types of insects spread quickly, and sometimes it is overwhelming.

But, this prevention is the answer. Nowadays, it has become very easier to prevent insects and control them from your Hydroponic garden.

Before knowing how to prevent and control the pest, you have to know about what are the common insect problems in Hydroponic?

6.2 Aphids

They usually find food around the stem and can be black, green, or greyish color. Aphids easily attack plants, which are weak or stressed. However, they are soft, pear-shaped insects with wings sap from all parts of the plant.

The worst thing is it spread the virus from one plant to another.

Prevention

The overfed plants are easily attracted to aphids. Always offer organic plant food to plants.

Solution

Use insecticidal soap to control aphids from becoming extra vulnerable.

Ensure that you will not bring anything from outside near to hydroponic plants as aphids are found in the outdoor environment.

6.3 Whiteflies

They look tiny moths and quickly fly away when you try to catch them. They suck the juices of the plant in every stage so that it will not grow.

Before they started feeding, they exude a sweet fluid, which is also called honeydew. The sign of the whiteflies can be seen when you see the mold on the leaves of the plants.

How to prevent it?

In your hydroponic grow room, you can release parasitic wasps, which mainly prey on whitefly nymphs. Time to time, you have to scrape the tiny eggs from below the leaves.

Resolutions

The solution for this is placing a few sticky traps which have the capability

6.4 Spider mites

They are very, very small in size, even more, modest than whiteflies, and are the most dangerous infestation for your Hydroponic system. They are of various colors like pale green, yellow, reddish, and they suck the juices of the plants from the stem.

If on the leaf top you can see the yellow speckles, then it is a sign of spider mites.

Prevention

They usually occur in dry conditions, so keep the humidity level up to 50%, which best suits for every plant.

Solution

Pyrethrin is a naturally occurring substance in chrysanthemums is recommended for organic farming. Its main work is to paralyze the bugs and stop spider mites feeding. Keep in mind that spider mites quickly go from one plant to another, so isolate infested plants as soon as possible.

6.5 Fungus gnats

Fungus Gnats is not harmful, but its larvae can damage the plants. It can be found in the roots of the plants. It looks similar to whiteflies, but their color is dingy gray.

Prevention

You can use moss or algae killing treatment to clear the algae system in which larvae can feed on them.

Solution

Try to capture the flying adults with the help of a sticky trap. Spray with a mixture of neem oil, pyrethrin, and insecticidal soaps.

Keep in mind that this insect can lay an egg on hundreds, so never ever ignore this issue of pest.

6.6 Thrips

Thrips look like aphids that turn the leaves into yellow or brown color. It is another juice sucker pest that mainly targets flowers, and if they feed on petals or leaves, they become dark and brittle.

They bore holes and usually insert their eggs in leaves and stems.

Prevention

Just shake the plant gently, which stirs up Thrips. It's egg look like a minor pimple on the leaves, so crush them with a finger.

Solution

It gets easily trapped in the sticky trap, so you can dispose of them by this method. On the other hand, you can use potassium salts acids, which easily wash them off from the leaves. Moreover, the life cycle of thrips is concise, so you have to repeat the application of salt 3-4 times within a span of 10 days.

Now you will come to know various preventive measures by which you can control these pests. They are: -

1. First and foremost, the thing you can do and which is also the best means to maintain a healthy garden is cleanliness.

2. Before entering into the garden, wash your hands and even coming between the crops.

3. In your Hydroponic grow area to remove all the dead leaves and debris, which are scattered as most of the insects and pests come on the dead and decayed matter.

4. If there is any dead plant or it is decaying with time, dispose of them off.

5. For your Hydroponic grow area, keep a separate set of tools like trowel or pruners. Most fundamentally, don't use these tools on your houseplants or plants which are outside as insects ride from plant to plant.

6. Clean the tools while dipping into the isopropyl alcohol.

Various other preventive measures which are very crucial: -

1. Keep the humidity of the place around 50-60% and keep the hydroponic garden cool that is 75 degrees.

2. There should be proper ventilation and regular air movement as it prevents mold and funguses.

3. Make sure you don't overwater the plants, which again can create mold, mildew, and algae.

4. When you are working on outdoor crops, never come directly to indoor plants. Instead, do it reverse.

5. Don't come directly to your indoor garden after visiting the plant nursery.

6. Don't smoke inside the grow room as plants can catch a virus.

7. Always use yellow or blue sticky cards so that you come to know the number of pests around the plants.

8. Ensure that when you enter the garden, always wear sterile clothes.

9. Don't bring anything into your hydroponic area, which is not clean or contaminated.

10. Whenever you are trying a new plant in the growing area, to be careful as it can bring various pests and insects with them as it is coming from outside.

What are the measures you can take if there is a pest or insects in your hydroponic growing area which can damage the plants?

If you have noticed that pests or insects are there on the plants, you need to fix it quickly; otherwise, it will harm the plants abruptly. However, once pests had made their way to the plants, it becomes challenging to mitigate the issue. The speed of pests or insects is so fast that if one plant is affected, another will for sure get affected.

1. Don't take care of the pest

Acting immediately will save your plants before it gets damaged.

2. Determine what type of intervention is needed

Some of the pests or insects can be taken care of as the environment changes, manly removal, various other methods, but some can only be banished only with chemicals. But make sure that you don't use chemicals into your hydroponic system.

3. Handpick them

Some of the pests or insects are very big as you can pick them with your hands like caterpillars, beetles, slugs. Try to squash them or drop them in soapy water.

4. Spray them with water

Few of the pests can easily be knocked with the help of water, but make sure you spray the water underside the leaves.

5. Try a pheromone trap

This trap is commercially produced by the people, which is coated with sex hormones and few fragrances by which small insects get attracted to it. This trap can only work in an indoor area, not in the outdoor garden.

6. Use insecticides or fungal spray

Make sure that you use the least toxic spray, which does less harm to the pests or insects as saving the environment is our priority.

7. Spider mulch

Another way to save your plants from pests or insects is by offering spider mulch to them to hide, which is made up of straw or dried grass. With this, every type of pest will be under control.

One crucial thing to be noted that while setting up, spider mulch is set around the plants but doesn't allow debris to accumulate.

Well, all the above prevention and control measures need to be implemented if you want that your hydroponic garden will not get any pests or insects. Moreover, any of the products which you are using on your organic plants should be branded in order to make them safe and healthy.

6.7 Pest Prevention and Troubleshooting

Unfortunately, when growing anything, there's a risk of encountering issues that hinder the quality of your plants. That being said, with hydroponics, it's fairly simple to prevent such problems arising, which will ensure you get your desired results!

It's vital to keep your growing area free of pests, and you will more than likely achieve this if you keep the growing area very clean. However, pests have a higher chance of becoming a problem when you're growing indoors - there are fewer natural pest preventatives (e.g. rainfall, birds etc.), so it's even more crucial that you keep your indoor growing area obsessively clean. Make sure to remove any stray mud, dead leaves, or any other excess debris.

If you're still one of the unlucky ones, then here are some solutions for the main growing issues.

Fungi and Algae:

Too much humidity in your growing area can give rise to fungi growth. It's critical that the correct humidity levels are maintained, and your growing area is supplied with a constant supply of fresh air. You should also constantly remove any dead stems or leaves from the area, and avoid excessive watering of the plants. But if you're unfortunate enough to experience a fungi outbreak, using a quality fungicide will be a viable option to solve the issue. If you can spot an outbreak early enough, then you'll have the chance to prevent further growth by carefully removing the fungi with a dry cloth.

It's important to be aware of other types of fungus that can become a problem in the growing medium. If you notice this, then use a layer of LECA medium on the top layer of your existing medium - this will help absorb any excess moisture.

Algae is another potential difficulty that thrives from receiving light. This can occur both in your nutrient solution reservoir and on the growing medium - it will compete for a nutrient solution which can deprive your plants.

Be sure there aren't any direct rays of light entering your reservoir and make sure the water is being regularly agitated. If this does occur significantly in your reservoir, it will need washing out with 1/10 concentration of bleach. If it occurs on the growing medium, be sure to completely wipe it away.

Pests:

Although we've already covered the preventative measures, we'll cover what you can do if you do end up with pests infesting your sacred plants. Many growers choose to use toxic pesticides - I don't recommend this as a number of bugs can develop resistance to them, which can make them useless. My favorite natural solution is to use sticky traps that lure in pests with bright colors and then trap them, making them a pest no longer! These can be easily made by using petroleum jelly spread on top of a blue or yellow painted cardboard strip.

Overall, make sure that you're very meticulous in constantly checking your plants and growing area - this will give you the best chances of eliminating any potential threats before they become a full-blown hindrance!

6.8 Other Techniques to Help You Maintain Your Hydroponics System

Here are a few hints on the best way to capitalize on your new development room.

1. Picking the Perfect Measure of Room for Your Plants

The main thing to remember before you set up your development room: the amount you will develop. When you have a smart thought of what number of plants will consume the indoor development room, you can decide how a lot of room you have to leave between the plants and the light source you will require.

2. Finding the Correct Gear

Utilizing the correct gear in your development room configuration can positively be the contrast between progress and disappointment.

Utilizing the right LED lights will help since the innovation in them is at long last, making up for the lost time to the lights most expert cultivators have utilized for quite a long time. Likewise, make certain to have a period change to consequently killing the lights on and for when your plants explicitly need it.

Your cannabis develops room can't flourish without ventilation. With no moving air, the plants will overheat and kick the bucket. It is ideal to utilize a wind stream framework and a fan for a predictable air course so the temperature and carbon dioxide will spread equitably all through the room.

At long last, a waterproof floor is significant in your development room arrangement and configuration just as an approach to check the stickiness. Having the appropriate measure of dampness noticeable all around will help the development of your plants, and yet guarantee there isn't an excessive amount of stickiness, which will avoid organism and form development. In the event that you need to go down the hydroponic way, it will diminish the requirement for pesticides and herbicides. Likewise, hydroponically developed plants become quicker and can lessen water utilization by up to 90% rather than ordinary agrarian strategies.

3. Give Appropriate Supplements to Your Plants

When planning a development room, make certain to utilize living or natural soil in your pots. As indicated by Cannabis and Tech Today, "Living soil is wealthy in microorganisms and microfauna, which separate supplements in the dirt and make them simpler for the plant to retain.

Natural soils and supplements are not just economic. Plants developed with these strategies will, in general, have more strong taste and flavor profiles than buds developed utilizing non-natural techniques."

Simply recollect that it will be critical to give nitrogen, potassium, and phosphorus for your plants. However, don't try too hard. Nitrogen lethality is excessively regular of ruin for producers.

4. Guarantee Your Plants are Sheltered and Secure

It ought to abandon saying that you won't be a fruitful cannabis rancher if your plants are devastated or demolished. When you investigate your develop room arrangement and configuration, are there enough bolts for the entryways? Are there, in any case, somebody who could vandalize the area? It may likewise be ideal to think about putting resources into cameras. It is an additional expense, yet it could wind up sparing you a great deal of cash contrasted with having your plants taken or devastated.

Those are only a couple of proposals on the best way to capitalize on your cannabis development room. Make certain to take a gander at all the various choices you have and choose what the best way for you to guarantee the most beneficial and most strong yields conceivable is.

Extra Equipment

Notwithstanding the fundamental hydroponic arrangement, it's a smart thought for learners to put resources into a couple of extra things.

You will need meters to test the PPM and pH of the water, just as the temperature and relative stickiness of the room. There are some mix meters accessible that will test the pH, PPM, and water temperature. You can likewise buy meters that measure the temperature and, additionally, the mugginess in your development room.

Contingent upon your atmosphere, you may require a humidifier or dehumidifier to change the relative dampness in the development space to an ideal level.

You might need to have some sort of fan or air course gear to improve the wind current in your development room. Indeed, even a basic swaying fan functions admirably, yet as you get increasingly experienced, you might need to put resources into a progressively refined admission and-fumes framework.

Chapter 7: What to Avoid

7.1 Mistakes to Avoid in Hydroponic Gardening

You will be able to produce more herbs and vegetables of better quality if you know beforehand the mistakes you can avoid in hydroponic gardening. It helps to closely look at nine of the most common errors and learn how to find your way around them:

- **Not Doing Any Research**

Growing your herbs and vegetables in a hydroponic garden is easy once you get the hang of it. But as a beginner in soil-less gardening, you need to arm yourself with lots of knowledge about the different aspects of a hydroponic garden. Failing to read up on all kinds of information about the different types of hydroponics systems or growing media, for example, can result in your failure to build your dream garden, even if you have all the materials required for the job.

- **Not Planning for Enough Space**

Ensure plenty of space for your herbs and vegetables to grow in. You might try using your backyard's unused shed to serve as a little greenhouse for your hydroponics plants.

- **Relying on Convenience**

Not everything named as a plant food can be used in making your hydroponics herbs and vegetables grow and thrive. You have to realize that nurturing a hydroponics garden is extremely different from tending a traditional soil garden. Aside from taking charge of the proper growing conditions yourself, you also have to take into account the proper ratios involve when mixing your nutrient solution. Always purchase your fertilizer salts and nutrients from reputable gardening centers and other authorized dealers of hydroponics gardening materials.

- **Depending Too Much on Artificial Lights**

Fluorescent lights are not suited for your hydroponics herbs and vegetables at all stages. They are needed most by your seedling plants, which will do extremely well with white light. As your hydroponics plants grow, they would need other light colors (such as blue, red, and orange), all of which natural sunlight can provide.

- **Neglecting the Plants' Needs for Adequate Air Circulation**

In case there is no getting around having to grow your hydroponics herbs and vegetables in a small grow space, consider using a blower or fan to prevent the deterioration of their health due to poor air circulation.

- **Applying Too Much Fertilizer**

Feeding your herbs and vegetables with too much fertilizer only causes salt deposits as well as fungus to build upon your hydroponics system's growing medium. This leads to stunted growth.

- **Overlooking the Importance of Proper Hygiene**

Know that wet floors are a big no in the grow space. The same goes for the accumulation of bacteria in your hydroponic system's reservoir and the presence of any non-sterile equipment or tool.

- **Harvesting Too Early**

While some types of herbs and vegetables can be harvested after only a few weeks from planting, it just might be best for you to allow all your hydroponics plants to reach their maximum growth before you consider harvesting them.

- **Not Finding the Right Balance**

You would not want to neglect your hydroponics herbs and vegetables, either. To achieve the right balance, you might visit your garden and check on its water level, pH level, air circulation, and other hydroponics factors once every two days.

7.2 Maintenance of Your Hydroponic Garden – Myths and Mistakes to Avoid

Regardless of why you want to enter the world of hydroponic cultivation for entertainment or for profit, you should know everything before investing in this business. Of course, every one method has downsides, but it's better to carefully familiarize yourself with many subtle points that you can easily manage. With proper planning and study, you can avoid many costly and time-consuming mistakes that can hit not only your wallet but maybe pride.

Mistakes and Wrong Thinking

1. Lighting savings

Many people are mistaken in thinking that fluorescent lamps are suitable for all plants at all stages of growth or are simply trying to grow on these lamps because of their cost. The truth is that fluorescent lamps emit only one kind of light: white. Sunlight, which is a necessary standard by which all other types of lighting are evaluated, emits the entire necessary spectrum of lighting. Simply put, fluorescent lamps are more suitable for young plants. As your plants enter the vegetative and blooming stage, they will need a red, blue, and orange spectrum of light, all in order to grow accordingly. Fluorescent lamps can cost you much more than you expect because they will yield a poor quality crop compared to other types of lighting lamps.

An excellent choice for lighting your plants is a full spectrum LED light or incandescent light. These are an excellent choice for the vegetative stage of growth.

2.   Wrong thinking means more is better

Water is necessary and beneficial for your plants in the same way as it is for you and me, but this does not mean that your plants will be glad that you are overfeeding them. If you give too much water to your plants, the roots will rot, and the plants may die. If you use too many fertilizer nutrients, you will get salt deposits on your growing systems that will slow the growth of your plants. Make sure that you spend the right intervals between watering time, so that the roots dry out a little, and always, always, always try to adhere to the feeding cards that come with the fertilizers.

3.   Thinking that any fertilizer is right for your hydroponic garden

A hydroponic garden is different from a traditional garden and, therefore, has unique needs. Always buy fertilizers and nutrients in specialized stores that sell everything you need for hydroponic cultivation, and even better. Many people who are not completely dedicated or who think that they are too smart may be tempted to simply buy a bag of fertilizers at a local hardware store, but this, as they become convinced over time, will only lead to big and unnecessary disappointment and most likely to kill your plant.

4.   Misunderstanding the pH problems of your nutrient solution.

Make sure that you understand what pH is needed for your crops, and of course, take the time and get a good pH meter. And if you adhere to all the recommendations, do not make ridiculous mistakes, you can say with confidence that growing on hydroponics is fun, as the result will amaze you.

Chapter 8: Nutrients during Seeding and the Cloning Procedure

- **Nitrogen deficiency (N)**

Yellow leaves can be a sign of a nitrogen deficiency. If nitrogen deficiency occurs, the plant will move the available nitrogen from the older leaves (bottom) to the new leaves (top). This means the bottom leaves will become yellow while the top leaves are still green. If you inspect the leaves carefully, you will see that the yellowing begins at the tip of the leaves, slowly making its way to the center.

- **Phosphorus deficiency (P)**

The leaves become darker, almost purple. The leaves will start to curl and will eventually drop. Phosphorus will be hard to spot at the beginning.

- **Potassium deficiency (K)**

Potassium deficiency is also hard to spot. Older leaves (bottom) will form chlorosis (yellowing), and the edges of the leaf will turn brown with sometimes brown spots in the middle of the leaf.

The flowering of the plant is greatly diminished.

- **Calcium deficiency (Ca)**

Calcium deficiency appears on new leaves. The edges of the leaf turn brown. Calcium deficiency is not to be confused with tip burn (too many nutrients) or lack of airflow.

It might be possible that your plants are developing signs of calcium deficiency even when there is enough calcium in the nutrient solution. This is because the environment you are growing in is too humid. The leaves cannot transpire water, which will lead to less nutrient uptake. One of these nutrients that fails to be taken up is calcium. Calcium is used to maintain cells. If calcium is not supplied, the new leaves will turn brown on the edges.

Decrease the humidity to fifty percent and install fans to circulate the air.

- **Magnesium deficiency (Mg)**

Deficiencies can exist four weeks before you could see it happen. The leaves at the bottom will start to yellow between the veins (interveinal yellowing) with brown spots forming on the leaves. Over time, the leaves will almost completely turn white.

The older leaves will dry and curl up, eventually falling off the plant.

- **Iron deficiency (Fe)**

Iron deficiency will lead to interveinal chlorosis at the new leaves (top). If you are using UV lights to remove algae from the water, you may have an iron deficiency. UV light makes iron precipitate out of the solution, making it unavailable for your plants to take up.

8.1 Too many nutrients

Too many nutrients can become a problem when you have nutrient build-up or just have added too many nutrients.

You should provide them with a quart or half of the dose of the mature plant.

Too many nutrients will result in nutrient burn, which are brown spots at the edge of the leaves. Not to be confused with calcium deficiency. The leaves will become dark green and start to curl up.

If your plants have nutrient burn, you need to flush them with a half-strength solution and lower the nutrient concentration.

8.2 The Cloning Procedure

To prepare your cutting, you will need to find a healthy plant and then remove the best-looking growing tip. There should be no more than two sets of leaves. If you plan on cloning tomatoes, use the suckers.

When removing the soon to be clone, you should cut at a forty-five-degree angle to increase its area of nutrient uptake. The clone needs this because it doesn't have roots yet. Allow two nodes on each clone. A node is a place where a leaf appears. You must remove the bottom leaves of the clone to increase its likeliness of developing roots.

Now place it into a cloning sponge. It will take between seven to fifteen days for the roots to develop.

Cloning sponges

When roots have developed, you can transplant them to your hydroponics system of choice.

The reason for leaving only two leaves on the clone is because the plant still evaporates water to continue photosynthesis. Because there is no root, the plant uptake of water will be limited. Reducing light during this stage will reduce the need for water. Only increase light exposure when roots are developing.

8.3 Making Clones of Your Favorite Plant

The second method of restoration is cloning. This technique takes a small rising tip from a stable, mature plant and creates its own roots. This approach is independent of the reproductive system of plants and removes the Possibility of future generations evolving as cloning results in plants that, in all aspects, are exactly the same. Cloning is very popular with indoor and sheep growers: who want to preserve the particular characteristics of a favorite strain. To properly cut into the heart, the following must be observed:

•	The temperature of the root zone 72 to 76 degrees Fahrenheit.

•	70 to 78 degrees Fahrenheit air temperature and 90 to 100% humidity.

•	Low-intensity ambient light (20 watts fluorescent).

•	Dilute solution root feeding. Rooting hormone can be used because it can improve the cuttings.

•	Dilute foliar feeding 20 percent nutrient strength spray.

Chapter 9: Macronutrients and Micronutrients

9.1 Plant Nutrition

Plants, like humans and animals, have very particular nutritional and environmental requirements that must be met to grow and develop the plant. Likewise, both humans and plants need to eat a balanced diet and protect themselves against hostile environments. It is essential to review the organic composition of plants to develop a solid fundamental understanding of hydroponics. And to do this, we need to consider what the elements are and how they are used for life processes by living organisms.

Scientists and researchers have determined precisely what and in what quantities a plant needs minerals. A large number of hydroponic nutrient solutions are produced, and there is no perfect mix, although some have better results than others. The effectiveness of each mixture of nutrients depends on the conditions in which it is used and which plants are being cultivated. Most hydroponic gardeners use a combination of pre-mixed nutrients to which they add just water. Such solutions contain in the correct proportions all the minerals and nutrients a plant requires and are available in powder or liquid form.

9.2 Macronutrients

Macronutrients are the substances consumed by the media in large quantities or, in our case, the nutrient solution. They are the best known and widely accepted constituents of plant food and are, as such, used as a handy guide to defining plant food potency.

- **(N) Nitrogen:**

Essential for the formation of amino acids, chlorophyll, and coenzymes.

Deficiency: lack of or insufficient Nitrogen (in the form of both nitrate and Ammonium) will result in plants with small yellowish leaves and spindle-like appearance. Some parts of the plant might end up having a purplish coloration.

Toxicity: Excessive nitrogen exposure will lead to excessively vigorous growth, dark green leaves, and delayed fruit maturation. Plants may also increase their susceptibility to pests.

- **(P) Phosphorus:**

Sugar production, phosphate, and ATP (energy)-the production of flowers and fruits-the growth of roots.

Deficiency: The deficiency of phosphorous causes plants to stall and turn dark green. Lower leaves are yellow and can assume a purple tinge as they draw phosphorous to feed new growth. Leaves will curl backward and drop when growing fruit, thereby damaging the root system.

- **(K) Potassium:**

Synthesis of proteins requires high levels of potassium. Rigidity, root growth, and sugar and starch production also require potassium.

Deficiency: Growth slows while mottling develops in the older leaves, and plants become fungus-prone.

Toxicity: Excessive potassium can result in a deficiency of secondary magnesium.

9.3 Micronutrients

Micronutrients are nutrients that are absorbed in quantities small to minute.

Below is a list of examples and their effects on plant's production:

- **(Ca) Calcium;**

Required for the formation of cell walls.

Deficiency: Deficiency of calcium causes leaves to stunt and crinkle. Young shoots die, and the plant's blooms fall. Calcium-deficient tomatoes will develop brown spots at the bottom of the fruit that will cause deterioration, especially when high temperatures begin. This is called end rot or BER in blossom.

- **Toxicity**: It is challenging to detect excessive calcium.

(S) Sulfur:

Synthesis of proteins, absorption of water, fruit, and seed acts as a natural fungicide.

Deficiency: The deficiency of sulfur is rare, but it can cause young leaves to turn yellow with purple bases. Toxicity: excessive sulfur slows the growth and produces smaller leaves.

- **(Fe) Iron:**

Formation of chlorophyll, which helps to generate energy through the respiration of sugars. Deficiency: Iron deficiency is quite common, causing new growth to pale and plant blossoms to fall. Initially, yellowing between the veins can be observed, and leaves may die along their margins. Toxicity: It's hard to spot excessive Iron, and occurrence is quite uncommon.

- **(Mg) Magnesium:**

Used in the production of chlorophyll and enzymes.

Deficiency: Magnesium deficiency triggers the curling of older leaves and yellow areas between the veins of the leaf. Only the youngest crops will remain green as Magnesium is moved to feed the new ones from the older plants.

Toxicity: The effects of toxic magnesium are rare.

- **(B) Boron:**

Necessary in conjunction with calcium to form cell walls.

Deficiency: Boron deficiency leads to weak growth and brittle roots. Stems can split and twist.

Toxicity: Excessive boron will yellow the tips of the leaf and cause them will die off.

- **(Mn) Manganese:**

A growth catalyst acts as a precursor for oxygen formation in photosynthesis.

Deficiency: Manganese deficiency causes leaves to yellow between the veins and leads to failure of blooms.

Toxicity: Excessive manganese may decrease Iron's availability.

- **(Zn) Zinc:**

Used in the production of chlorophyll, respiration, and metabolism of Nitrogen.

Deficiency: zinc deficiency causes small leaves with crinkled margins.

Toxicity: too much zinc can also reduce Iron's availability.

- **(Mo) Molybdenum:**

Metabolism and fastening of Nitrogen.

Deficiency: There are small, yellow leaves with signs of weakness.

Toxicity: In rare instances, excessive molybdenum may cause tomato leaves to turn bright yellow.

- **(Cu) Copper:**

This element activates the enzymes needed for metabolism and photosynthetic processes.

Deficiency: Copper deficiency leads to pale, yellow-spotted leaf stains.

Toxicity: much exposure to copper can also reduce the availability of Iron.

- **(Co) Cobalt:**

Cobalt is not known to be needed directly by plants, but nitrogen-fixing organisms that support legumes such as beans and alfalfa feed require trace amounts of Cobalt. Cobalt is also found in vitamin B-12, which is essential to all life forms. As additional research is carried out, there may be more to come on the subject.

Chapter 10: Equipment Needed

10.1 Irrigation

One of the key factors to a hydroponics system is its water supply. Getting the correct nutrient-to-water solution balance is imperative to the growth of the plants and crop production.

Most hydroponic systems work on a recycling principle where the water stored in the reservoir is pumped from the tank to the plant's root system. Once the roots have taken their share of the moisture, what is left over is usually drained back into the tank or cycled off. Most hydroponic systems that do not use the recovery cycle only feed the plants the amount they need, which tends to leave little to no waste runoff.

A lot of hydroponics irrigation systems also tap into natural water sources like natural drain runoffs or rainwater tanks. Hydroponic innovative irrigation systems make it possible for arid countries to farm-fresh produce.

The irrigation management in hydroponics is a bit more complex than soil-based systems as the water needs to be constantly monitored for its pH and nutrient balance. The irrigation is usually on demand, and because of it being a root based system, any sudden changes in the irrigation schedule could do harm to a plant or an entire crop.

Irrigation is generally held in a specific tank that has a balanced amount of nutrients-to-water volume that is required for the nourishment and watering of the plants. The water-nutrient solution is then pumped to the plant's roots by means of a submersible pump held in the reservoir. The water is dispersed by means of some form of hose, sprinkler, or misting system. Or the plant roots are suspended in the water-nutrient solution and oxygenated by an oxygen-stone in the water tank.

There are many different irrigation schemes that work well with hydroponics, aeroponics, and aquaponics. But it is all classified as on-demand irrigation with the plant's water needs determined by its type and environment, such as temperature, vapor pressure, and humidity.

10.2 Pots and Trays

Each hydroponic system has its own pots and tray requirements. They can differ quite drastically depending on the hydroponic system type. There are six different types of hydroponic systems.

Pots

The pots are either solid pots with large drainage holes at the bottom, they can be soft and flexible or hard and solid.

Which one you choose depends on what it is going to be used for and is also based on your personal preference.

Pots that are used for systems such as deep water culture, Nutrient Flow Technique, and vertical gardens use netted pots. These are best for systems that require the roots to be free of medium and accessible to the spray or water solution.

Deep Water Culture (DWC)

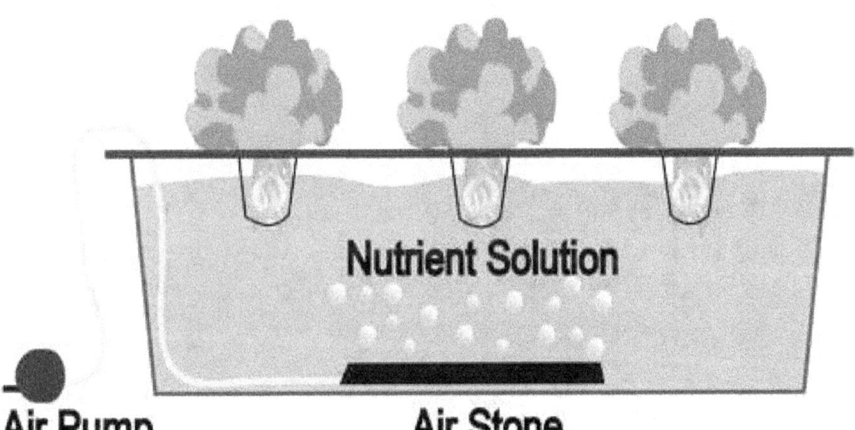

Pots are chosen to accommodate both the size of the plant and the hydroponic growing system. They must be able to fit in it comfortably without touching another pot on the grow tray or grow tube.

They are usually double the depth of the grow tray, and no more than the recommended number of pots for your system should be placed on a grow tray at any one time. This is to ensure that the plants are being fed the correct nutrients and

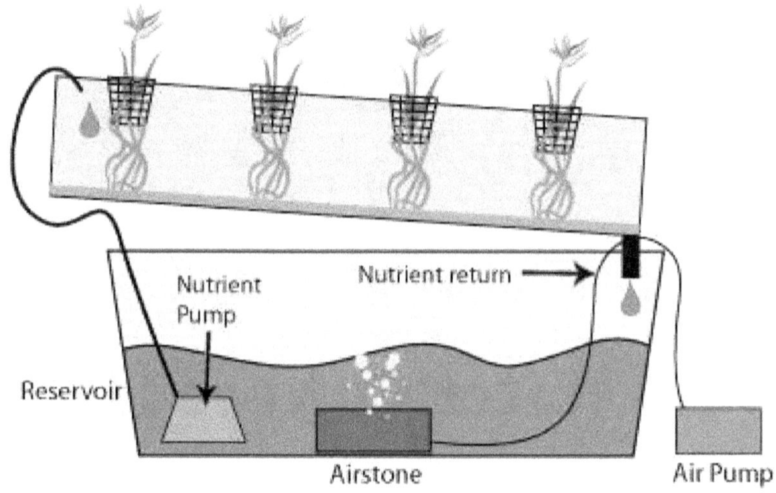

to promote optimum growth and yield.

Trays

All hydroponic systems need some form of grow tray, lid, or tube upon which the plant either stands in a pot or netted pot and is suspended over the water or encased in a grow tray.

The trays come in many different shapes and sizes, which cater to a wide variety of different plants as well as the different hydroponic systems. These trays usually have sections where the pots stand, and an inlet and outlet opening for the feeder and drainage pipes.

The tray should be the same size, if not slightly bigger than the reservoir tank, and the plant capacity should never be exceeded.

Trays are usually made out of some form of plastic, polystyrene, or PVC.

10.3 Growing Lights

Hydroponic lighting can be quite costly but is needed in a growing house-type environment. These lights are specifically designed to give the plants the exact lighting they need for the daily maximum required time.

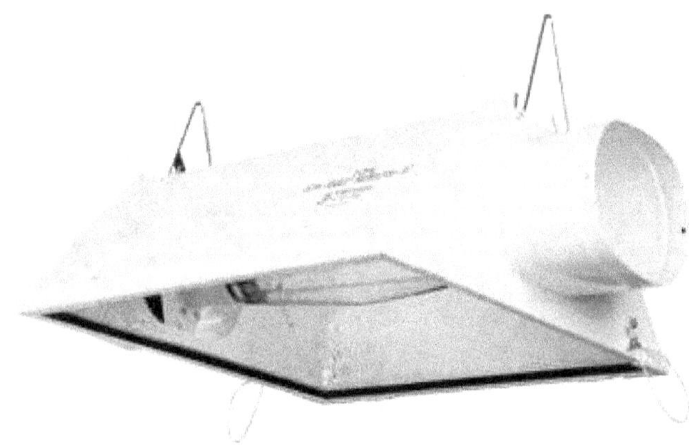

Normal vegetable plants require up to 10 hours of light a day, which can be both indirect and direct sunlight. For indoor hydroponic gardens, a grow light that can mimic something close to this is needed. The lighting system will need to be on for at least twelve hours a day.

An automatic timer is needed to make this a lighting system; one that is energy efficient is always the best idea. The grow lights that have automatic timers can be a bit pricier than the manual grow lights, but they are well worth the investment. Without automatic lights, you could lose an entire crop over one forgetful moment.

Before going out and investing in a grow light, it is important to do some homework first.

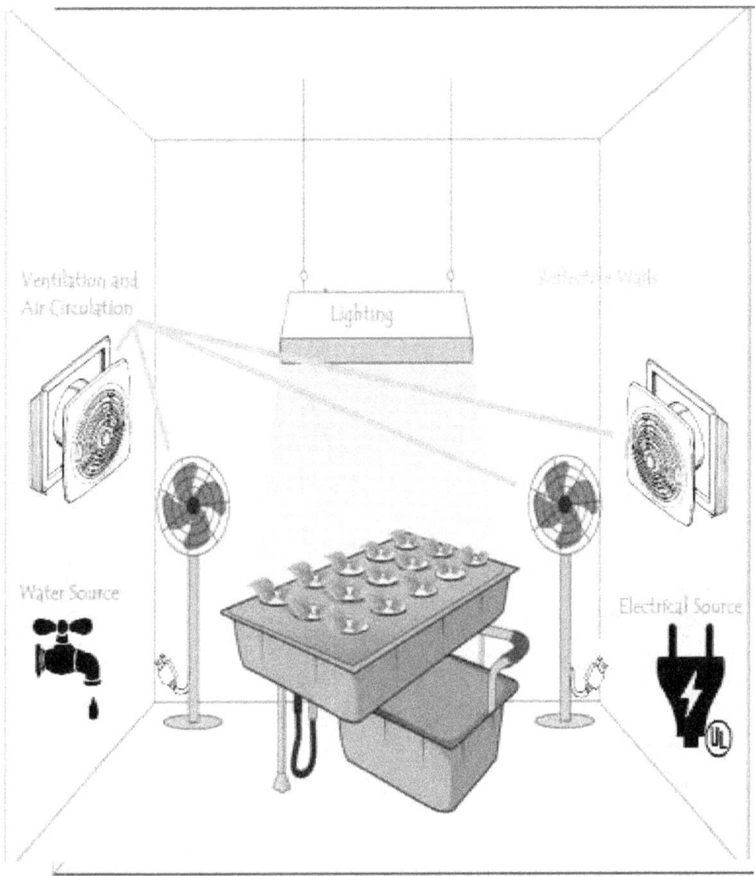

The type of light you need will depend on the plants that are being grown, as some plants may need a bit more sunlight than others and so on. For a mixed garden, this will get a little more complicated.

Before investing in a grow light, make a list of the plants that are going to be grown in the hydroponic system. Then check how much recommended daylight they require. From this, a person can start to work out what schedule their plant's lighting system will need. Once a person has a clear cut vision of how and when the light is going to be used, you will have a better chance of choosing one that is right for your growing environment.

All of the components of the grow light must be chosen carefully for your environment. These all have to be taken into account when buying a grow light.

The three main parts of a grow light are the bulb, the timer, and the remote ballast.

The bulb

Actually, this is one of the most important parts as it is what determines the quality and brightness of the light for your grow room environment. Another important factor to take into account with the bulb is how energy efficient it is.

Hydroponics usually need a bulb that is around 400 - 600 Watts.

The preference is an HID (High-Intensity Discharge) light, which produces a nice pure white light that is the closest to actual sunlight.

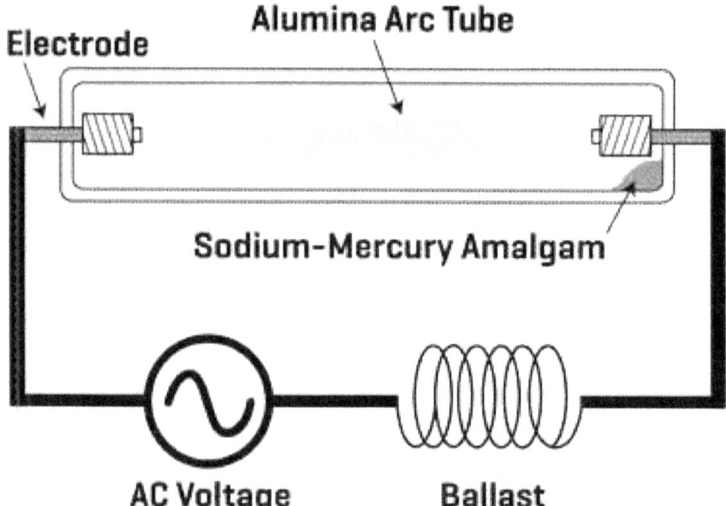

Conversion lamps can easily switch between the two types of bulbs available, which are the Metal Halide and High-Precision Sodium bulbs.

The High-Pressure Sodium bulbs are better suited for plants that are starting to flower in the fruit-bearing stage. These bulbs tend to last the longest out of the two types but are also more expensive.

Metal Halide bulbs are the most commonly used and can be used in nearly all hydroponic growing applications. They provide an adequate lighting situation for most crops and will need to be replaced every two years or so as they tend to start to lose their power at around fifteen months or so.

If you can afford it, these two work very well in conjunction with each other.

Timer

Although the lights with timers do seem a bit more expensive, the timer on the lights is not that expensive and can actually cost a lot less than the actual bulb itself.

There are two types of timers, manual and automatic. The manual types use pins to set them. The manual timer tends to be a bit harder and less prone to going wrong or breaking than the automatic ones. They can also be attached to two different lights at the same time. This makes them the more popular choice of the two.

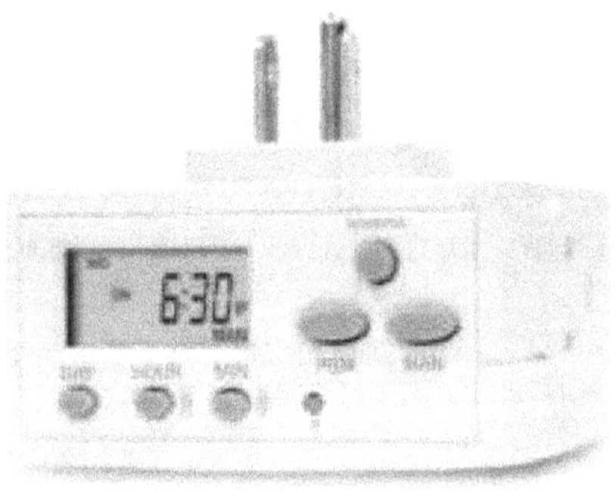

Automatic timers are prone to breaking, going wrong, and if there is a power outage, they won't work. They may seem a bit more convenient than the good old fashioned manual ones, but they can also be a bit more troublesome as well as expensive.

10.4 Remote ballast

This is the box that powers the fancy grow light. They are heavy and very susceptible to moisture, so they should be kept above ground level at all times and far away from water or damp conditions.

They are usually sold as a set with the bulb because the ballast has to match the bulb in order to effectively power it. They are usually only used in home system environments.

10.5 Substrates and Growing Media

Hydroponics is the growing of plants without soil and using a water-nutrient solution to feed the roots. But some of the system types still need materials to help anchor plant roots, absorb moisture, or provide drainage. This is called a growing medium or substrate. There are different kinds of growing media, and the ones you choose depends on the hydroponic growing system being used.

Growing media is divided into different types:

- Organic Growing Medium
  - Coco Coir
  - Peat Moss
  - Pine Bark
- Foam Matrix
  - Rockwool
  - Oasis cubes
- Grains and Pebbles
  - River Sand
  - Pebbles

- Lightweight expanded clay aggregate
- Perlite
- Vermiculite

10.6 Equipment for Growing Indoors

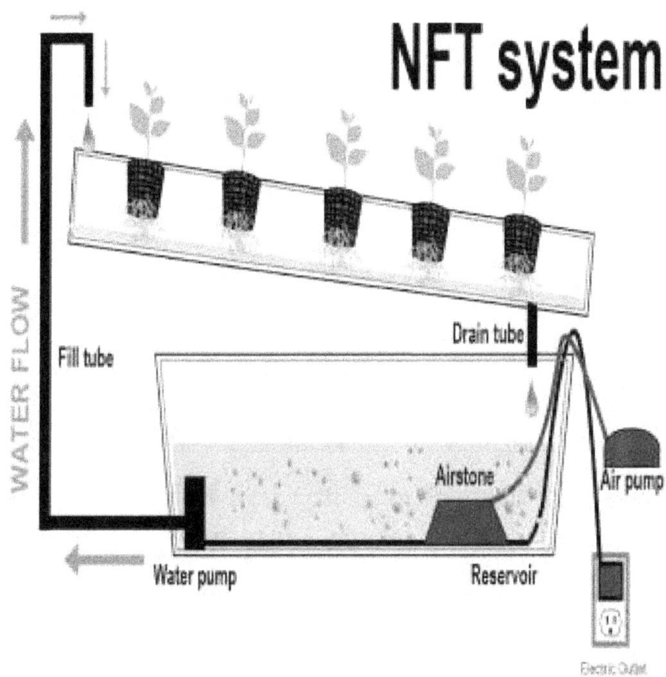

The indoor equipment for hydroponics is pretty much the same as it would be for the larger hobbyist. Only not on such a large scale.

Many of the hydroponic systems come with ready to assemble kits complete with:

- Growing medium

- Nutrient solution

- Pumps

- Tubing/pipes

- Water Nozzles/sprayers/hose pieces and piping nipples

- Grow Tray(s)

- Reservoir Tank

- Grow Pots

- Set up instructions

The above kit is generally the basis for most of the six hydroponic systems and can be used both indoors and in grow tunnels and greenhouses.

You may need to add a grow light, decent pump, and an oxygen stone, but that is about it.

The kit size will depend on the plants that are going to be grown.

All the hydroponic systems can also be done DIY style, and most of them are not that hard to make as a DIY project.

The trick is managing the water to nutrient balance, the pH balance, and getting the temperature, humidity, and lighting just right. But these things take practice to master, and everyone has to begin somewhere.

10.7 Meters

The hydroponic system relies on the quality of the water-to-nutrient solution ration and the pH balance of the solution. Sometimes these values will fluctuate and become a little out of bounds. This is normal, especially when the system is a recovery system that recycles the nutrient solution. Each time the solution is used, the plants extract nutrients from it. It also affects the pH balance of the water. The two main levels that need to be constantly tested are the pH and EC levels.

These can both be done quite easily with meters or one meter that can test both.

pH

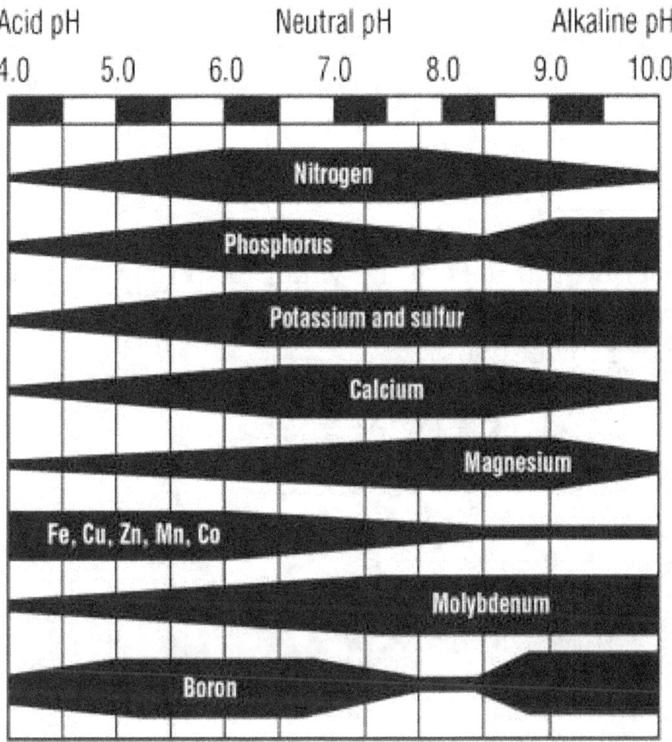

Effect of soil pH on the availability of plant nutrients

This is what determines the acidity level of the water solution. It also demonstrates how various plants are reacting to the nutrient mix and how various other organisms are affecting the system.

Each growing environment has its ideal pH range in which it can function normally—kind of like testing the levels of acidity in a swimming pool to keep it clean and clear. For instance, a good example of an optimum pH range for the growing of leafy greens and herbs would be around 5.5. In order for it to maintain a good balance, the pH level should not move beyond or below .5 each day.

The pH rarely rises in a hydroponic system. It is more common that it will drop. To adjust the pH solution, you may need to simply apply a base solution to the mix.

EC

This is the level of nutrients in the water (also known as the salts in the system) and should be kept within a range of no higher than 2.0 or lower than 1.2.

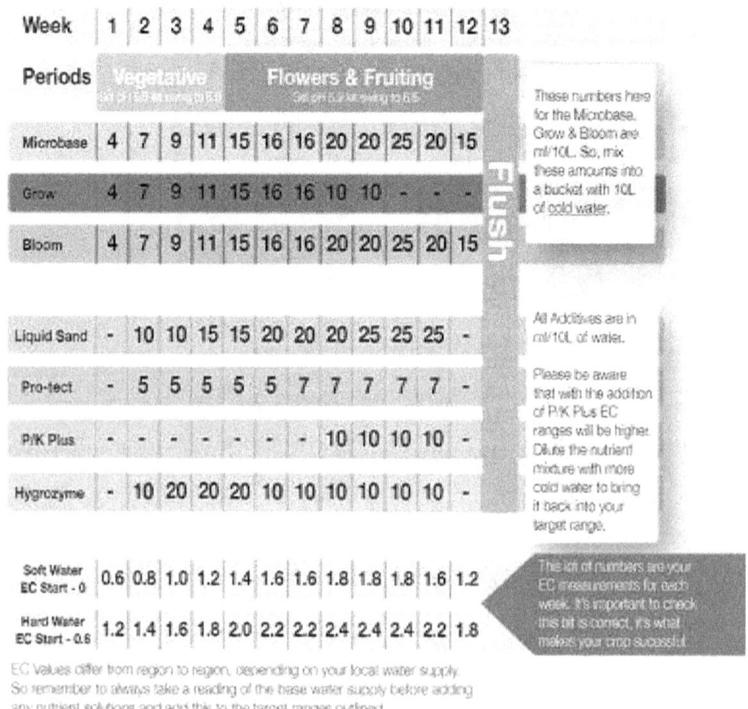

Week	1	2	3	4	5	6	7	8	9	10	11	12	13
Periods	Vegetative				Flowers & Fruiting								Flush
Microbase	4	7	9	11	15	16	16	20	20	25	20	15	
Grow	4	7	9	11	15	16	16	10	10	-	-	-	
Bloom	4	7	9	11	15	16	16	20	20	25	20	15	
Liquid Sand	-	10	10	15	15	20	20	20	25	25	25	-	
Pro-tect	-	5	5	5	5	5	7	7	7	7	7	-	
P/K Plus	-	-	-	-	-	-	-	10	10	10	10	-	
Hygrozyme	-	10	20	20	20	10	10	10	10	10	10	-	
Soft Water EC Start - 0	0.6	0.8	1.0	1.2	1.4	1.6	1.6	1.8	1.8	1.8	1.6	1.2	
Hard Water EC Start - 0.6	1.2	1.4	1.6	1.8	2.0	2.2	2.2	2.4	2.4	2.4	2.2	1.8	

EC values differ from region to region, depending on your local water supply. So remember to always take a reading of the base water supply before adding any nutrient solutions and add this to the target ranges outlined.

If the EC solution is too high, you simply need to add more fresh-water to the reservoir until the level evens out to a more acceptable level. If it drops, you will need to add more nutrients to the mix as per the manufacturer's recommendations.

EC and pH Meters

You can get individual meters to test each one, but it is more economical and easier to get a dual meter. The dual one can quickly help a person determine what needs to be adjusted in order to bring the pH and EC levels back within an acceptable range.

10.8 Delivery System

Plants in a hydroponic system rely on three things to help them grow:

- Water

- Nutrients

- Oxygen

There are six different hydroponic systems, each offering a different delivery method of these three elements to the plants.

These six systems are:

- Drip Hydroponic Solution: This delivers a steady drip of solution directly to the root of each plant by means of a dedicated nozzle.

- Wick Hydroponic Solution: This system uses an absorbent wick type rope, string, or felt to suck up water to the root system.

• Nutrient Film Technique: In this system, the roots of the plants are constantly in touch with a thin nutrient film that is set to constantly flow over them.

• Ebb & Flow System: As the name describes, in this system, the plants are flooded to a watermark with nutrient solution pushed through on a timer then drained until the roots dry out.

• Water Culture System: Here, the plants are floating on top of the reservoir with their roots in constant contact with the nutrient solution.

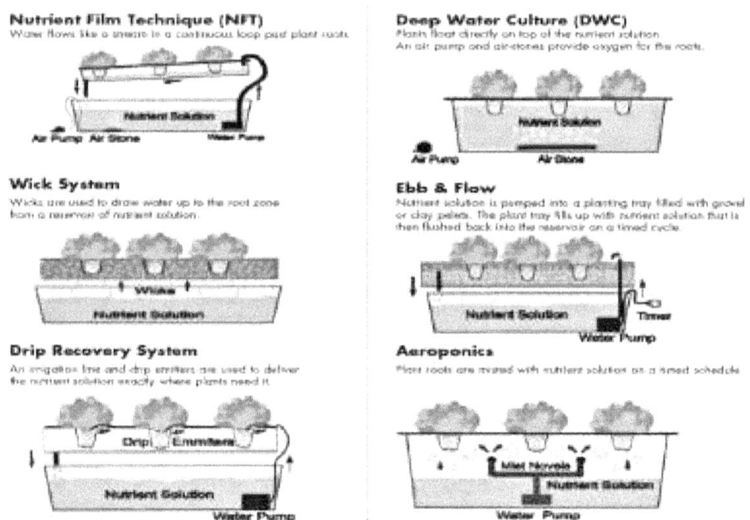

• Aeroponic System: With this system, the plants are suspended, and their root system is subjected to a light spray of nutrient solution.

10.9 Timer

There are different types of timers that are available for hydroponic systems, from the easy manual pin timers used to control the smaller grow systems to large, sophisticated ones that are used by commercial farmers.

Timers give growers more environmental control over their grown rooms. This is a piece of equipment every hydroponic grower will eventually invest in, especially indoor growers.

There are timers that are used to control the lighting, and then there are the timers that are used to control room ventilation. Then there are those that are used to control the nutrient solution dispersal intervals. This is perhaps the most important of all the timers as it is the one that determines when and how long the garden gets watered for.

Before you even look at buying a timer, you should invest in a power strip that has a really good surge protector. This is also a necessary piece of equipment that usually gets overlooked until it is too late.

The type of timer will depend on the hydroponic system being used. It will also be dependent on the type of plants being grown and how often they will require nourishment.

The timer will be something that is chosen once the size and type of hydroponic garden have been determined, along with the plants that are to be grown. This does not have to be anything fancy. It can be a standard mechanical timer as long as it can operate in the needed time frame.

10.10 Pump

You get air pumps and water pumps with a hydroponic system.

Air Pumps

Usually, a standard airstone attached to a pump is enough to aerate the reservoir tank and feed the plants. When buying an air pump, it should be able to generate at least 500 ccs of air per minute.

The general rule of thumb is that for every 1 gallon of water in the reservoir tank, there should be at least 1 watt of power.

Water Pumps

There is no precise way to choose a water pump for a hydroponic system. The only thing to be aware of is that getting one that is a bit too big is better than getting one that may be too small. You can adjust the flow down on one that may be a bit too big, but you cannot increase the flow on one that may be too small.

The pump will be determined by the type of hydroponic system that is being used. The thing to keep in mind when choosing a pump is how high the pump needs to push the water to its designation. Once that is determined, a person will have a better idea of how powerful a pump is needed.

Most pumps will need to be water submersible as they will sit in the reservoir, and for smaller systems, usually, a standard fish tank pump is adequate.

Chapter 11: Starting Your Seeds

It is most satisfying when you plant a seed and nurture it until it becomes a full-grown plant and provides you with the intended harvest.

Of course, it takes more effort to grow a plant from seed than it does from a seedling. You need to decide if this is your preferred method and discover the best way of starting seeds.

Hydroponics is an excellent system for starting seeds as you have complete control over the elements your seeds are exposed to.

11.1 Seeds vs. Seedlings

For your first attempt at hydroponics, it is quicker to plant seedlings. However, controlling all the elements of the growing process includes controlling the seeds. If you decide to plant seeds, you will have complete control over the type and quality of the seed you plant.

Put simply, you can have any variety of seed but not necessarily any variety of seedling. Seeds are generally easier to get hold of then seedlings.

The other consideration is the growing media. In hydroponics, you avoid using soil. However, unless you have a hydroponic center near you, the seedlings you purchase are likely to be grown in soil. This means carefully removing the soil to avoid contamination of your system. Unfortunately, washing them can damage the roots of the seedling.

Besides, seeds are cheaper than seedlings, allowing you more opportunities for failure without breaking the bank.

With proper planning and equipment, you are better off growing the plants from seed.

11.2 Starting Your Seeds

The best way to start seeds is to use a seed starter cube. A cube, the size of one and a half inch, will fit perfectly in a two-inch net pot. These small cubes are capable of holding water while air can reach the roots, which is the most important while germinating seeds.

First, you need to soak your grow cubes in chlorine or chloramine free water with a pH of 5.5. Water from your tap will be around 7-8 pH. You most likely need to use a pH down solution.

Getting the chlorine out of your tap water is quite easy. Let it sit for one day for the chlorine to evaporate. If you want it to evaporate faster, you can use an air stone to air the chlorine out much quicker.

If your water company uses chloramine, you need a reverse osmosis filter to remove the chloramine. Note that not every reverse osmosis filter can remove chloramine. Chloramine can't be aired out and needs to be filtered. If you do not have a reverse osmosis filter available, you can use one thousand mg (one gram) of vitamin C (ascorbic acid) per forty gallons (one hundred and fifty liters) of water.

Use a tray to soak the cubes, pour the water on top, and let it sit for a few minutes. Once most of the water is absorbed, you need to drain the rest of the water. Do not squeeze the cubes. This will remove air pockets inside the cubes.

The next step is dropping your seeds into the holes. This can be a big task if you need to do a lot of seeds. Commercial growers use pelleted seeds and a vacuum seeder to speed this process up. Pelleted seed is a seed that is wrapped in clay. It is bigger, thus easier to handle.

You could also use a toothpick and dip the tip in some water. This will make the seed stick to the toothpick, as shown in the following image.

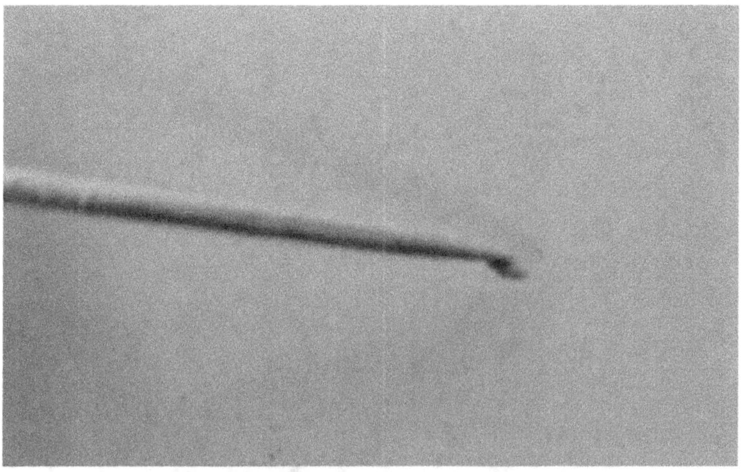

Using a wet toothpick to pick up seeds

Placing the seed into the seed starter cube

If the holes of the grow media are preventing you from dropping the seed in, use a pen or a toothpick to open the hole back up.

You can use more than one seed per hole if the germination rate is bad. I always use two seeds per hole. When both seeds germinate, I keep the best one and use scissors to remove the bad one.

Next, place your humidity dome on top of the tray to keep the seed starter cubes moist. Generally, the seeds don't need water until they have germinated. If you notice that your seed starter cubes are drying out, you can pour some more water in

the tray. Don't forget to drain the rest of the water.

Rockwool cubes with seedling

Image from a bootstrap farmer

Once the seeds start showing its first two leaves, you need to put it under a light source. This will provide the plant with the energy they need to grow. If you experience that the stems are growing long (stretching). It means that your plant is reaching for the light. Increase the light on the seedlings to avoid this stretching. Do not use the red light on seedlings. White fluorescents that are 6500K are perfect.

After ten days, you can transplant them to your system. If you are growing in a greenhouse, it can take fifteen days in winter.

Heat mats will increase germination during colder weather. The mats are placed under the seedling tray to warm up the seed starting cubes. Setting the heat mat to 68°F is recommended.

Recap:

1. Soak your seed starting cubes in chlorine or chloramine free water. Distilled water is even better. Make sure the pH is around 5.5.

2. Put the seed starting cubes in a tray.

3. Put the seed in the holes of the seed starter cubes.

4. Cover the seed starting cubes with a humidity dome.

5. Set the heat mat to 68°F (20°C) and place it under the tray.

6. Once sprouts appear, water them from the bottom with one quarter nutrient strength. The cubes will wick up the water.

7. Place them under T5 fluorescent lights. The humidity dome is still on the tray.

8. When you see four leaves and the roots are developing out of the seed starting cubes, it is time to transplant them to your growing system.

Nutrients during seeding

Seeds don't need nutrients initially as they are self-contained. However, you can give them a quarter-strength solution, compared to what you are using in your adult plant hydroponic system.

11.3 Cloning

When you hear the word 'cloning,' you probably think of science fiction and all sorts of adverse outcomes when humans mess with the natural order of things.

However, plant clones are used a lot around the world. In essence, a plant clone is simply cutting from a plant that is allowed to grow by itself. The new plant has the same characteristics as the original plant. Cloning can be used to ensure all your plants have a good yield. Take your clone from an existing plant that yields highly.

But, it is more than just an efficient way to get healthy, high-yield plants. Cloning is considerably faster than purchasing seeds.

Of course, successful cloning takes a little more knowledge than just planting. You will need to make sure the conditions are just right.

- The roots temperature should be around 68°F (20°C).

- Air temperature should be 64-77°F (18-25°C).

- The light must be diluted and never direct.

- You only need a partial nutrient solution. Use twenty-five percent of the standard recommended nutrients for the plant.

- You can use rooting liquids like clonex from hydrodynamics to help the roots to become established.

Chapter 12: Germinating Seeds and Transplanting the Seedlings

The most initial step in your plant growth is seed germination. The success of seed germination determines, to a great extent, the health and growth success of your plant. Thus, it is important to ensure that seed germination is given due preparation and desired attention.

When a seed begins to germinate, the roots begin to come out of the bottom of the seed, and the shout starts to come out of the top of the seed. This makes the plant seedling, which will become the plant you are growing. Most of the time, people germinate the seeds in the soil, but with hydroponics, it is a bit different.

Always start the seeds in a dampened, growing medium. It is best when the growing medium is damp and not soaked. The depth to shoot for is about 1/8' inch depth. Some seeds are different; for instance, Lettuce just barely needs to be covered, and the same goes for Basil. It is best to research the specific seed and the right depth it needs.

In most cases, the seedlings will be ready to be transplanted in about two weeks. If this is being done indoors, they can be placed at a window that gets a good amount of light that comes through it throughout the day. Fluorescent Grow Light can also be used. It is best to keep the fluorescent grow light a couple of inches above the seeds. The best temperature for this is around 70-80°F. You do not want them to be too hot, or they will burn up.

A good root system is important before transplanting the seedlings. When the seeds are about 2-3 inches high, you should start to see the roots coming out, then they are ready to be transplanted.

12.1 Types of Growing Mediums to Use When Germinating Seeds

Germinating with Rockwool: Germinating your seeds hydroponically can be done in various ways. One way is using Rockwool. There are Rockwool cubes that are made for germinating your seeds. The best sizes would be 1 inch or 1.5-inch cubes. If your Rockwool dries out, you can lower the plant container in the water tray. If you are using a timer, make sure it is working properly. Sometimes it can get off time. You can also check the hose to the water and see if it is connected properly.

Germinating with Perlite: You will need a tub or small container and fill it Perlite or Vermiculite. Perlite seems to be the better of the two because it does not mess with the PH Balance and creates air space. You can place the seeds in rows, or however you would like as long as they have enough space from each other to grow. It is best to not go more than two inches deep when putting the seeds in the Perlite.

Starting the seedlings in root cubes: This is a great way to start multiple seeds at once. The root cubes are a tray that you place the seeds into. The tray is made of multiple cubes, and you place a seed into the hole of each cube.

Starting the seedlings with plug trays: Plugs trays are different from root cubes because you will need a growing medium. The plug trays come in different sizes; the most commonly used size is the #50, which means it has 50 plugs to start seeds into. You can use many different growing mediums.

Starting with dome and heat pad: These are starter kits that you can purchase. There is a plant tray with a dome top, and underneath is a heating mat. Also known as a propagation dome. They do come in different sizes. Instructions should come with the starter kit you purchase. Another option is to use tuber-ware with a lid and place a Hydroponic Heating Pad underneath.

Can you transplant plants from soil? The answer is yes. Just wash off the roots and get all the soil off first.

12.2 Process of Germinating the Seeds

Materials required

- Seeds
- Hydroponic cloner
- 2-inch net pot

- Starter plug (preferably Rapid Rooter)

- Air pump

- Airstone

- Tubing

Procedure

- Get your materials ready

- Fill your cloner with water – tap water can do well.

- Insert air stone into the reservoir and connect the tubing. Plug it in and switch on to test. Switch off after testing

- Soak the starter plugs into water. Once properly soaked, place it into the net pot.

- Insert seeds into a starter plug. For vegetables such as cabbage, eggplant, broccoli, tomatoes, basil, peppers, and cucumbers; plant 2-3 seeds per plug.

- Place the plugs in the nursery tray.

- Water daily by adding a seedling solution to the drain pan (not the cubes/plubs).

12.3 Process of Transplanting the Seedlings

Preparing to transplant

1. Make sure that the hydroponic infrastructure is well set and working

2. Make sure that the grow-on medium is properly set and ready

3. Make sure that the following environmental conditions are appropriate:

- Light control

- Aeration control

- Grow-on medium

- Temperature control

- pH level control

- Nutrients

4. Start hardening off your plant

5. Prepare the seedbed

Hardening off

Survival mode enables them to easily adapt to a new environment with minimal shock, if any.

The following are some of the ways to harden off your seedlings;

- Prune excessive branches

- Gradually reduce the amount of light

- Gradually cut down on the amount of nutrient consumption

- Gradually increase or decrease the amount of water consumption so as to match the consumption expected of the new environment

- Gradually adjust the temperature to match that of the expected new environment

- Gradually adjust pH level to match that of the expected new environment

Preparing the Seedbed

- Immediately prior to transplanting, dig up holes within the grow medium wide and deep enough for the entire plug to be inserted.

- Have sufficient material to support the plant once transplanted

Transplanting

- Carefully take the hardened-off seedlings in their starter plugs from the tray and insert them into the already dug holes in the seedbed (net pot).

- Support the transplanted seedlings with appropriate support material of the respective grow medium.

- Set the hydroponic system in motion (pump on, light on, etc.) so that the plants can start receiving nutrients and continue in their growth path.

Chapter 13: There are different types of Growing Hydroponic System

The way to culture plants on the water varies from one method to another, and this is usually seen in the type of equipment that is used to grow the plants in water. A little more information will be dropped.

13.1 Aeroponics

This system would usually need only the air and the nutrients to thrive. The crops are planted or instead suspended on the tray, which would contain water. It will also contain some nutrients at the base of the system. The roots of these are usually misted with some nutrients and water that would mix after every minute. This is let down through a nutrient pump. For an ideal practice, it is advised that plants be protected from pest and disease, as this would help accelerate its maturity. Hydroponics is used alongside with Aeroponics, and it is often referred to as the crop saver. In situations where the Aeroponic system fails, the hydroponic system stands as support supplying the plants with nutrients. This type of system has particular applications in large business ventures as it can stand harsh conditions.

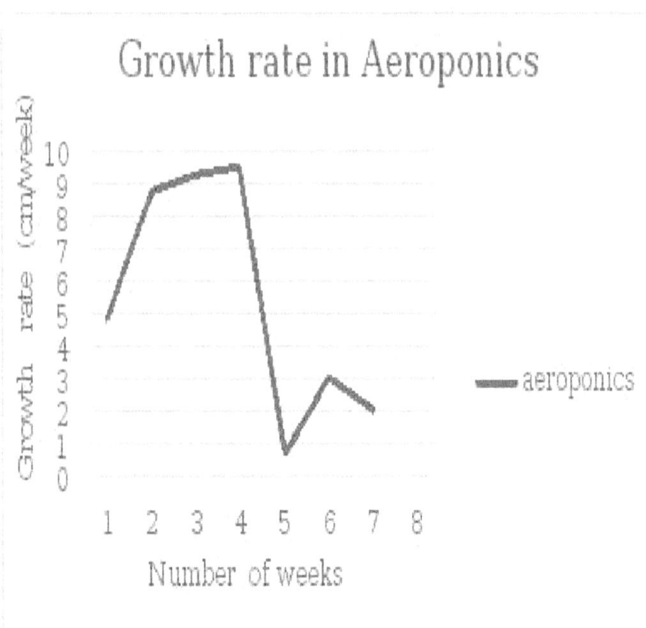

13.2 Drip System

This system is one of the widely used hydroponic systems. It comes with Nutrient-rich water that is usually pumped through small tubes at the root of the plant, and this moves towards the top of the plant; it has a timer that controls the submerged pump. This kind of hydroponic system is perfect for plants that are smaller and do not have a developed root system. The drip system increases crop yield, and this sometimes because water is retained for a longer period of time as opposed to being lost through evaporation. This saves water and has been known to prevent the growth of weeds. It encourages farming at all weather conditions, even during drought. Another attractive feature of the drip system is the reduced need for pesticides and fertilizers, which may be harmful to the environment. The drip system though not fully explored is a cost-effective environmental friendly way of farming

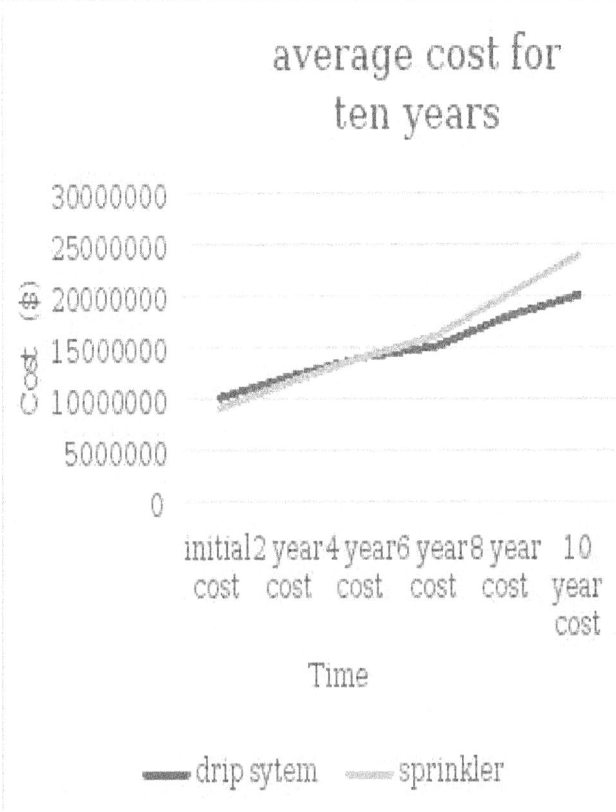

13.3 Ebb and Flow System

This system requires a reservoir (buckets, water bottles), a container which would be used for growing plant roots, a pond pump, a pump timer to turn the pump off and on, a tubing system that connects the pump in the reservoir to the system and another that drains back to the reservoir and a tray. Different designs exist for the Ebb and Flow System; depending on the materials available, you can have your stem set up. The containers in series design, flood tray design and serge tank flood and drain

For the flood tray design, the plants are usually in a basket or any preferred container is placed on the tray, and it is temporarily flooded with the nutrient solution from the reservoir; the tubes are placed at opposite sides, and this is done to ensure that the nutrients solution pump circulates before draining to the reservoir. This is then drained into the reservoir where it is recycled. The timer that is attached to this system helps to control the pump to do an excellent task all the time of the day. Gravels or perlite are used to provide the necessary stability that the plant needs. It is suitable for home use too.

This method is highly flexible and gives room for garden alteration at any point. The challenging part of this method comes in the assembling of the instrument, and once this is done, every other thing becomes easy. Cleaning is important for this method of the hydroponic system because algae tend to grow on this surface, which may eventually lead to mold, use up the oxygen in the system, and insect infestation, which is then harmful to the crops. Algae growth is almost inevitable for this method of the hydroponic system because the top of the tray is left open and gives room for sunlight, which promotes the growth of algae.

A container in series design allows for different containers to be used at the same time. There is a tubing system that allows for all the containers to get nutrient solutions at the same time. It also has an overflow tube like the tray design used to take excess nutrients back to the reservoir.

The surge tank flood and drain, just like other ebb systems, has its reservoir lower than the flooded areas of the system. Now with the aid of gravity, draining is made a lot easier and faster.

This is the most expensive of the flood drain system because of the complex equipment used. Water is pumped from the reservoir into the surge tank, the tanks nutrients solution to all the containers evenly till the water level is high enough. At this point, water is pumped back to the reservoir from the tank, the pumping continues until the water level is low enough, the timer goes off, and the valves are shut up. The serge system works because water has a way of balancing its level.

13.4 Nutrient film technique system

The Nutrient film technique system is quite popular amongst farmers who grow baby greens, lettuce, and different types of herbs. There are different system designs for this system, but they all share some things in common; the root system is in contact with water descending from a connected tube.

Some of the instruments needed for the Nutrient Film Technique includes a reservoir, a pond pump, a tubing system, and some small baskets.

For this system, plants are supported in a small plastic basket that is placed in a tray where the roots are being hanged in the air in a nutrient solution. The pond pump sends nutrient solutions to the tubing system, which is arranged such that the solution flows downwards in a fixed direction. The only part of the part directly in contact with the nutrient solution is the roots. The other part of the plants is suspended in a way that prevents them from the reservoir. The roots get nutrients when a thin film of the nutrients solution passes through the basket, excess nutrients which are not absorbed flow back to the reservoir through the tubing systems.

This particular system is created to give a consistent flow of solution over the plant roots. This solution is then taken off into the reservoir. This system is best for a plant that has extensive root systems such as tomatoes.

13.5 Water culture system

This hydroponic system is almost the least complex amongst all the hydroponic systems but still grows plants effectively. Its setup is also cost-effective, and this is because it is not complex at all. For the set up you need a reservoir to store the nutrients solution, an aquarium air pump, a hose to channel the nutrients solutions, air stones to create bubbles, containers like baskets, pots to hold the plant, and a conducive environment to enable the plants to grow properly. This system is known as the Styrofoam platform; it contains nutrient-rich water that holds the plant. The plant is placed in such a way that it allows it to rest directly above the reservoir; sometimes floating Styrofoam keeps the plant from sinking in, sometimes the roots are passed through openings created in the lid of the reservoir. There is an air pump that provides the air that bubbles it with the aid of the air stones. These bubbles are important; they help the roots get oxygen and air and prevent it from suffocating, and also helps in the provision of nutrients and the supply of oxygen. It can be used for just a few types of plants, such as lettuce.

13.6 Wick System

The simplest of all the hydroponics system is the wick system. It works without air pumps and electricity. It works with an optional air pump and air stones. The system has no parts that are moving, with the medium being perlite or rock wool in the tray, a container for the plant, reservoir, and some good wicking rope.

A good wicking rope should be able to absorb nutrients and moisture at a very fast rate. Testing the wick for absorbent rate is good practice, also test to see the rate at which it rots. When you are done testing, wash the wick and reuse it. Wicks that have been washed have a better absorbing quality than newer ones. Blanket strips, strands from the mop head, wool felt, and cotton ropes also form good wicking material. Feel free to use any of this if you find it difficult to get results from the test. In getting a reservoir, whether large or small, ensure that the water level is close enough to the root system. High water levels help the wick deliver nutrients quickly because if the short travel time. To avoid algae buildup, the reservoir would require cleaning from time to time.

The nutrient is then released slowly into the tray through the wicks. This kind of system is better than the rest because it does not require any timers or pumps. This system is highly relevant for places that experience unstable electricity.

Some heavier feeding fruiting plants grown in this system (though simple to build) may suffer from malnutrition stemming from the speed at which the wick delivers nutrients to the roots. These heavier feeding plants require nutrients faster than lighter feeding plants, so for the wick system, it is advisable for users to focus on lighter feeding plants. The wick system is easy to use but can be disadvantageous when it comes to using it with larger plants. This is because larger plants take in a lot of water to enable them to grow properly. Another downside that goes with this system is the uneven absorption of nutrients and water by the plants with the wick constantly taking up water and nutrients at the same time. Over time this causes a buildup of unused nutrients in the reservoir, and determining the exact amount of nutrients needed may be tedious. Getting rid of this buildup will require flushing with plenty of clean water.

Chapter 14: What are the common mistakes Hydroponic beginners commit?

Read about common mistakes which most of the beginners commit while starting a Hydroponic system, which can damage the whole crop.

If you are very fond of starting a Hydroponic garden, then you have to take things relaxed and sluggish. However, Hydroponic is one of the great ways to grow plants at home, but it can be challenging side by side and fun and rewarding too.

There is a varied number of issues which Hydroponic garden can encounter, so it is very crucial to understand and try to avoid them for the betterment of crops.

The gardening of Hydroponic is a very technical process by which plants will grow. There are countless books, videos, and articles related to the Hydroponic system, which can be beneficial for individuals who are going to start their hydroponic system.

If you talk about mistakes, it is a human nature that occurs intentionally or intentionally, but sometimes the result can be dangerous. However, you can be perfect by learning from your mistakes.

But why are you focusing on your mistakes?

Let's come forward and face it so that it will not happen next time. Mistakes and failures make you successful in your life. Have you ever talked to the most successful farmer? You can notice that he sees every error as the opportunity so that he learns from every small mistake and improve it.

As a beginner in hydroponic farming, learn from every mistake to be an expert in it. Now, you will come to know the varied types of mistakes that you can do while performing a hydroponic system.

14.1 They are as follows: -

Ignoring the PH level: The PH level of the plants is the most crucial factor which cannot be neglected at any cost. Every plant exists on the nutrient solution, and if that solution is too acidic or alkaline, the plants will face nutrient deficiencies, or they can die.

Get top brand PH meter and monitor the PH level of the plants every day means any time of the day. If the slider moves one direction, you have to take a mandatory step to balance it.

In reality, all the plants live in the same nutrient level, so if one plant suffers from a deficiency, all the plants could face it.

Thinking more is better: Water and world-class quality fertilizer are suitable for the plants, but it doesn't mean you will overload the plants with both of them. Offering too much water to the plants is not ideal for plants, as the roots will rot, and subsequently, the plants will die.

On the other hand, if delivering much fertilizer to them, you can see that the excess amount of salt will deposit, and fungus will grow. Ensure that you will offer an adequate amount of water and fertilizer to the crop and follow the instructions properly.

Don't use cheap and unreliable equipment: While doing hydroponic gardening, don't install cheap hardware such as timers, fans, lights, etc. Fine, your budget is limited, but don't compromise on various things that are going to benefit plants.

If you buy cheap equipment, then they need more repair as they get stuck in between but, if you purchase quality things, it will work for a more extended period of time and offer high growth to the plants.

Buy a good lighting system: Spending money in the right type of lighting can make or break your hydroponic garden. If the lighting is little, then plants will suffer. Buying the wrong kind of bulb for the crops won't allow them to grow. Purchasing a cheap bulb will not perform well.

In a hydroponics system, lighting plays an essential role, so research thoroughly with various stores and then make a decision. Moreover, don't think that the light which is coming from the window is sufficient for efficient growth.

Don't use the wrong fertilizer: When the plants are grown in the soil, there is an endless number of nutrients that are already present in the soil in adequate quantity, which is very helpful for the growth of the plants.

So, while buying the fertilizer for hydroponics plants, make sure that it should be appropriate; it means it doesn't have any traces of micronutrients.

On the other hand, you can make your own fertilizers with the help of scratch.

- **keep everything clean**

The first step towards healthy hydroponic plants is cleanliness. If you let your setup messy and dirty, it surges the risks of diseases, pests, insects to the system.

There are different things which come in cleanliness like keeping equipment clean and of good quality, stop algae, if you see the pests on the plants, take immediate action as soon as possible.

Most fundamentally, not only the hydroponic setup but instead also keep the surrounding area clean.

- **Growers confuse themselves with biological viability with economic viability**

Among beginners, there is a misconception that if you are starting a farm business, it 90% growing and 10% selling. But it is the opposite, and because of this, a farmer makes a few mistakes.

Firstly, they don't know the exact time and cost involved to make the crop accessible in the market; that's why in order to sell their produce, they don't have adequate time.

Latterly, they don't know the feasibility of the crop against the market. This means the plant they are growing, meeting the demands of people.

In this, the money they have spent in world-class equipment etc. goes in vain as no one is ready to buy their yield.

- **Not monitoring the overall health of the plants**

Observing the plants from time to time is the crucial factor that must not be missed by the grower at any cost; otherwise, you will lose the early sign of problems which plants are suffering.

Whether there is an insufficient growth or any signs of deficiency or any type of disease, the earlier you see that by regular monitoring, there are more chances of correcting them.

If you see any kind of issue with the plants, immediately try to find out the problem with the help or themselves and correct it on time; otherwise, it will ruin the whole crop.

- **Building an inconvenient hydroponic system**

There are countless things that can be very inconvenient to the hydroponic system. They are: -

- The setup is in less space without sufficient room for work

- Don't have suitable water resource for plant

- There is no adequate DIY system which is prone to leak or failure

The only solution to this can be, you don't need to want to start a hydroponic system at a significant level; start with small. Enhance your experience in the first few years and then enlarge it. The main reason behind this is, if you make wrong choices at the outset, there are chances your next conclusion is outstanding.

- **Not checking the installed equipment**

There are various things which you forget to do while doing hydroponic gardening like, forget to plug the water pump, not checking the growth of the crop, every installed thing is working correctly or not; otherwise, plants will suffer, and your money gets wasted.

Every time when you visit the garden, double-check the equipment and its settings.

- **Not focusing on sanitation**

Make sure that your hydroponic garden will not become a garbage bin. The sanitation habits which you have a significant and esteemed effect on the overall health of the plants, and you can say the entire hydroponic system.

Some of the basic cleaning needs you should address are: -

- Keep the floors of the hydroponic system clean and dry

- Make sure that you should sterilize and clean every system equipment

- Clean and sterilize every tool

- Every container which is used in the hydroponic system is adequately cleaned and sterilized

- Dispose of the plant waste regularly

Without proper sanitation, there is a chance of spreading various diseases and pests, which can ruin the overall crop.

- **Not trying to learn anything**

The system of hydroponic is evolving in this world around the 20th century, and at that time, there is lots of information that you can get with regards to the hydroponic system. The end number of colleges taught about it, and books are also available to fulfill the dream.

As a beginner in the hydroponic system, you can gain lots of information so that your hydroponic system will grow at a fast pace without any restriction.

Make sure that you will learn each and everything rightly regards the hydroponic system so that your investment will not go in vain. Indeed, learn from every mistake you do so that next time it will not happen again, and your hydroponic system will make you proud of what you have done to make the crops worth.

Chapter 15: Tips and Tricks to Growing Healthy Herbs, Vegetables and Fruits

15.1 Growing Plants on the Walls of Moss

The legendary Babylonian queen Semiramis left a descendant of the seventh wonder of the world - the fabulous "hanging gardens." Today, every amateur flower grower can successfully compete with Semiramis. However, to successfully compete with Semiramis, he must know how to build vertical (in the literal sense of the word) beds. This opportunity is given by the plant culture on the walls of moss.

Walls of moss, possibly the most original way to grow plants without soil, is a variation of the method known widely in the Republic of South Africa under the name and is widely used in this country. According to this method, these plants are grown not in a purely nutrient solution or on an inorganic substrate, but in an organic filler, that is, on suitably prepared plant materials, periodically moistened with a nutrient solution. From South Africa, information about this method reached Switzerland, and here, the method was picked up and developed with great imagination with many successful options by several people. With the help of some simple base (frame), the old horizontal bed is turned into a vertical one. This creates an ideal opportunity for the best use of space to accommodate the cultivated area.

The first attempts to grow useful plants on vertical beds were made in 1941, during difficult times. They wanted to know if it would be possible to grow more fresh vegetables using this method.

Basically, all the experiments gave a positive result, and nevertheless, despite these promising results, the culture of plants on the walls of moss until today has not found recognition in industrial vegetable growing, but it has found a greater response to amateur gardeners. An attentive observer every year sees more and more flower walls glistening with colorful paints in gardens, on terraces, balconies, flat roofs, etc. And this is not surprising...

15.2 The Basis

Before we start tinkering with something, we should outline the basic principles of the method in a few words.

The thing is to firmly hold, using a suitable base, in a vertical position, a moisture-absorbing organic substrate, which should simultaneously serve as a source of nutrient solution and a medium for the growth of plant roots. The filler in the finished base, or substrate, is periodically moistened with the prepared nutrient solution. Planting or sowing seeds is carried out through the holes in the base on all available vertical and horizontal surfaces.

Common in some places, the so-called strawberry barrel is the simplest suitable base. Any barrel that is unsuitable for anything else is suitable here unless it has been used before to store materials harmful to plants (chemicals, paints, etc.). In the walls of the barrel, drill holes with a diameter of 4 - 5 cm at a distance of 15 - 20 cm from one another. Only at the bottom of the barrel do they leave a belt of 15 - 20 cm wide intact. Before filling the barrel with a substrate, a small hole is drilled in its bottom through which excess liquid can flow. For the same purpose, large gravel is used, laid on the bottom of the barrel with a layer 1 cm high.

Now stock up on an empty tin can and a bunch of brushwood or a bunch of twigs. We put the jar (it should be 15–20 cm high) in the middle of the gravel layer and vertically set up a bunch of brushwood or twigs, and fill the rest of the barrel space to the top with a substrate.

Barrels prepared in this way are planted mainly with strawberries, which preserve decorative qualities throughout the growing season and, in addition, continuously produce fruit.

The substrate is poured with a nutrient solution from above, using a watering can, and the brushwood in the center of the barrel ensures a quick and even distribution of the liquid. Finally, a small bar is nailed at an angle above each hole to drain rainwater flowing down from above. The finished barrel can also be painted with oil paint, choosing a color to your liking. After painting, the barrel is completely ready.

15.3 Vertical Hydroponics

We now turn to the form that is probably used most often, namely the wall. The materials necessary for the construction of the first small experimental walls can be collected without much labor and almost without cost, especially if you delve into your own pantry. Metal rods, planks, slats, trim boards, a few nails and a bit of wire, and maybe the old wire mesh, you can probably find anytime, anywhere.

A prudent amateur will, first of all, think about the pre-treatment of building material. It is highly advisable to impregnate lumber with a substance that protects them well from moisture in order to protect them from rapid destruction. It is strongly recommended that you carefully paint over all metal parts (nets, wire, rods) with ordinary bitumen paint. This is done not only to protect against rust but also because, as it turned out, metal parts not coated with paint can react with a nutrient solution, as a result of which substances very toxic to plants can pass into the solution. This, of course, must be prevented. Therefore, you should choose only such means of impregnation and insulation, which certainly do not contain plant poisons (paints, which include the so-called heavy metals, are extremely toxic).

If the proposed structure, for example, for the garden is stationary, then four poles are simply driven into the ground in the right place and, you set them at the same height, connected for greater stability with rails of the appropriate thickness. Then the foundation is ready.

If it is planned to put a flower wall on a terrace, in a garden or elsewhere, then, of course, the portable base must meet these requirements. Therefore, we first build a solid base in the form of a wall about 50 cm long, 50 cm high, and 30 cm wide.

With such dimensions, a wall completely planted with plants will weigh about 65 kg and can still be carried.

As a next step, we will take care of limiting the side surfaces, and here you can go in different ways. It is very advisable to make a crate of narrow vertical rails with a distance between them of 5 - 7 cm. In this case, with the usually observed subsidence of the substrate mass, plants already planted between the planks will not be damaged. Since the mass of the substrate moistened with the nutrient solution is heavy, it accordingly exerts considerable pressure on the side rails. In order to prevent the strips from bulging out on more or less high walls, a reinforcing horizontal bar should be strengthened every 40 to 50 cm on the side surfaces, which, in addition, is connected by a wire to a similar bar on the opposite wall of the base. If this is done, then you need not worry about the side surfaces.

Another, often chosen and leading to the same goal, is the use of wire mesh. Any nets with mesh sizes from 50 to a maximum of 75 mm are suitable for this if they are coated with an insulating layer of bitumen paint. The advantage of nets is that after a short time, they become invisible to the eye since a thin wire is immersed in the mass of the substrate or masked by plants. The disadvantage of the grid is that when the mass of the substrate settles, the plants in individual cells are suspended on the grid and are damaged.

However, this can be avoided with a sufficiently careful filling of the mesh with a substrate. Lateral swellings are especially easy to form on wire meshes, so you need to take care of suitable screeds.

15.4 Hydroponic "life hacks."

Separate barrels or walls are planted with plants from above or from all sides. By this, however, the choice of forms is by no means exhausted. You can easily build planted columns, half columns, cubes, as well as arbitrary shapes like trellises, pyramids, garlands, hanging curtain rods and pots, etc. There is no need to dwell on the manufacture of the basis for all of these forms. Therefore, we confine ourselves to only general provisions for all forms.

When choosing a shape and determining the size of the frame, you can more closely follow personal tastes and adapt to the particularities of the place. However, it is always necessary to reckon with the following: plants must have a sufficient volume of substrate for the roots and have a stock of the solution corresponding to their size and number. The height and length of the structure can be chosen completely arbitrarily, but the width (thickness of the substrate layer) must have the following minimum dimensions: when planting with plants on all sides - at least 30 cm; when planting with plants on one side - at least 18 cm.

If this condition is met, you can be sure that the supply of nutrient solution to the plants is enough for 8 to 10 days.

We have already seen that vertical beds or walls can be stationary or mobile. They can even be put on wheels. In order to use the terrace as a flowering screen in accordance with the position of the sun, an enterprising gardener built several metal frames that could be made together like building blocks and made of the large floral walls. When decorating the stage, stands, and assembly halls, they always successfully replace the slightly treasured greenery of palm trees and evergreen shrubs.

Various vertical walls can also be used to decorate walls and parts of buildings. They can be suspended at any height, and the rear surface adjacent to the walls of the building can be impermeable to moisture (for example, from tin coated with an insulating layer, or from the roofing material, roofing felt, or plastic film) so that the walls of the building do not suffer. It is very advisable to put a couple of bars between the back surface of the base and the wall of the building, which will provide better ventilation.

Here, by the way, it should be noted that it is already possible to obtain bases made industrially from asbestos cement or metal. Since they are in good shape and made very reasonably, they certainly deserve attention.

15.5 Gardening Tricks

A wall of moss or peat can also be used for internal gardening. However, in this case, it is necessary to provide some kind of receiver to drain a possible excess of nutrient solution. The receiver can be a painted tin can or even a plastic tub installed under the base or suspended from it. With a known dexterity, you should immediately make a device for draining the liquid - it can be a faucet or just a siphon tube. If all this is provided for, we can be calm for the completely modern conditions for indoor plants that have been created.

Here, in fact, all the most important guidelines that must be observed when building the foundations for growing plants on a substrate of moss or peat. It should only be recalled that when planting young plants, you need to take into account the space required for a fully developed plant.

For example, if a fully planted foundation should ultimately have a length of 2 m, then a 2.6 m long frame is sufficient because the height of the plant on the end surfaces will be at least 0.2 m.

In conclusion, another indication for the site owner demanding on himself familiar with the craft of a bricklayer: a flower wall can be folded out of brick, or better yet, of uncut stone. To do this, first lay the foundation with a width of about 60 cm and the desired length. The top of the foundation is leveled, and a groove is made in it to drain excess fluid with an inclination to one side.

There is no need for the whole process of work; you should only warn that cement should not be saved. The strength of the structure will increase if you use a solution with a narrow ratio of sand to cement (2: 1 or 3: 1). When the masonry is finished, you need to hold the brush and cover the inner surface of the masonry and the top of the cement, i.e. all surfaces that will come in contact with the substrate, bitumen paint, to prevent the influence of lime or bricks on the nutrient solution.

A layer of coarse quartz sand with a thickness of 5-8 cm is first poured into the finished base. It will ensure the rapid removal of excess moisture. Then the substrate is stuffed, which should be much moistened to speed up the process of natural subsidence. After this, you can start planting the plants.

Another important point! You can greatly facilitate your work if, at the beginning of the masonry, at the end of the wall above the lower end of the gutter, several stones or bricks are fixed so that they can be easily removed. Then, using the poker, you can easily dig out the substrate from the usually inaccessible narrow space. Another detail: curly seams made of white cement give a special decorative effect to a wall made of bright red facing brick.

Using this method, you save the most space and get the most yield from your hydroponic garden!

15.6 Q&A

What is hydroponics?

Even though we have already covered this, for the sake of making it simple, we will discuss it again.

Hydroponics means working with water. Thus, it is the art of cultivation or gardening in which you are supposed to work with water instead of soil. Water is used in any form of gardening, but it plays a very important role here because hydroponics is gardening without using any kind of soil and done just using water.

Why do people fail?

Normally a person fails in hydroponic gardening because he or she has no knowledge of this system. Most of the time, these people are ignorant of the science behind this system and thus fail to get any yield. Another major reason is the lack of patience and discipline. Hydroponic gardening is not a hard system, but it is definitely a delicate system of gardening. A person needs to be very punctual and disciplined to get a good yield from this system. The final and also the most common reason why people fail with hydroponic gardening is the lack of ability. Do not get me wrong, everyone can do hydroponic gardening, but there are certain skills and characteristics such as determination, patience, effort, good working etiquette, etc. that a person needs to develop to be successful in hydroponic gardening.

Is your produce dangerous?

According to many home hydroponic growers, people still need to take caution when it comes to consuming hydroponically-grown food.

Many of the healthy food products that indoor growers produce, such as lettuce, herbs, salad greens, and wheatgrass, are included in the high-risk category of foodborne diseases. That is because most of these foods are consumed raw, with people veering away from the traditional way of killing bacteria, which is cooking.

What is cloning?

Cloning is simply the process of cutting a stem tissue or a leaf from a plant and then turning it into another plant. Because it is taken from a particular plant of your choice, you can be sure that the result of the clone will have all the desirable traits that you want in the new growth.

Why hydroponics?

As the world population has been expanding, there has been an increased need to produce more food, which led to the development of modern industrialized farming. Modern agriculture has lived up to its promise of increased production because there has been a greater supply of fresh, cheap, and nutritious food compared to the past, and its effects have particularly been felt in the developed world. However, modern farming has also brought with it challenges such as the promotion of waste, pollution, and increased strain on resources.

Conclusion

Hydroponics is quickly picking up force and prevalence as the most ideal approach to develop everything from flowers and nourishment to medication. Hydroponics is currently broadly acknowledged by shoppers and is rapidly getting on in different nations around the globe. At this point, you ought to be well on your approach to reaping your first harvest of hydroponic produce. Since the Hydroponic business is still relatively small, and there aren't numerous neighborhood shops at which to buy supplies.

This is a simple-to-follow, bit by bit manual for growing natural, solid vegetables, herbs, and house plants without soil.